# Fun With Worldbuilding

## Build Believable Worlds for Fiction and Nonfiction Writers

The *Write Boost* Writing Series

Karina Fabian

Laser Cow Press

MERRITT ISLAND, FL

**Laser Cow Press**
**Merritt Island, FL**
**https://fabianspace.com**

Book Layout © 2017 BookDesignTemplates.com
Cover art by Karina Fabian using ChatGPT for the image
This book was made with the assistance of ChatGPT based on author speeches and notes and was extensively rewritten.

**Fun With Worldbuilding: Build Believable Worlds for Fiction and Nonfiction Writers/ Karina Fabian** — 1st ed.
ISBN 978-1-956489-29-3

To Rob Fabian
*You are my world.*

*This tremendous world I have inside of me. How to free myself, and this world, without tearing myself to pieces. And rather tear myself to a thousand pieces than be buried with this world within me.*

– FRANZ KAFKA

# Contents

INTRODUCTION

# You're Already Building Worlds

That's a relief, right? *You're already building worlds.* But what does it mean?

When people hear the word worldbuilding, they tend to picture fantasy authors hunched over sprawling maps, inventing kingdoms with apostrophes in their names and sweating over trade routes. Or science fiction writers calculating orbital drift and effects of gravity on a planet's trees. Or someone explaining, with great seriousness, why their invented language requires a dental click.

All of that counts.

But it's not the whole story.

If you're writing a cozy mystery set in a small Illinois town, you're worldbuilding. If you're writing about the Ford Motor Company during the Great Depression and you bring in labor unrest, family tensions, and the looming shadow of war, you're worldbuilding. If you're writing memoir and evoke the feel of a childhood kitchen—the cracked vinyl floor, the hum of the refrigerator, the rules about who could sit where—you're worldbuilding.

Worldbuilding isn't about dragons.

It can include dragons. In fact, my own dragon, Vern, believes that dragons can only make a world better. But they're really awkward in outer space, and if you include them in a real-world news story, people start asking if you've taken your medication.

The point is, at its heart, worldbuilding is about context. It's the shaping of time, place, systems, culture, and physical reality so that the reader understands not only what is happening, but where it's happening and why it makes sense. It's what keeps events from happening in a blank room.

Without that grounding, story feels thin. With it, even the improbable can feel solid.

## The Jovian Problem

Years ago, I read a science fiction novel featuring a character from Jupiter. The author's primary adjustment for this character's origin was that he was shorter and stronger than humans from Earth.

That was the extent of it.

Now, I don't pretend to be an astrophysicist, but even I know Jupiter's gravity is crushing. If someone evolved under that pressure, "short and strong" probably wouldn't cover it. What would that gravity do to bone density? To movement? To architecture? Why doesn't every chair he sits in splinter?

The idea itself wasn't the problem. It was the lack of follow-through. One visible trait had been altered; the rest of the world remained untouched. The result: It felt incomplete and left me with questions and a feeling of dissatisfaction.

At the opposite end of the spectrum, there's Terry Pratchett and his Discworld—a flat world riding on the backs of elephants who stand on a cosmic turtle swimming through space. It is, on the face of it, absurd. Yet while you're reading, it feels completely believable.

Not because it obeys our physics. It doesn't try to. It works because it *obeys its own*. Plus, it affects everything from astronomy to politics to economics, even the history and culture. The premise may be outrageous, but the world is coherent.

One story adjusted reality and stopped. The other built a system and committed to it.

That difference is worldbuilding.

## What It Quietly Accomplishes

When worldbuilding works, readers don't usually notice it. They simply feel that the place exists. They trust it. They stop questioning how things operate and begin paying attention to the people living there.

That trust comes from coherence—when gravity affects more than height. When magic has limits. When religion influences daily life. When technology shapes social structure, or a historical event casts a long enough shadow to matter.

It also comes from restraint. You may know the full history of a city, but the reader only needs what the moment requires. They want to discover the world the way they discover a person—through interaction, not a résumé.

The balance between depth and discretion is part of the craft, and we'll return to it often.

## This Isn't Only for Speculative Fiction

Science fiction and fantasy make worldbuilding visible because the differences are obvious. Two moons require explanation. Psychic bonds between species require thought (in more ways than one). If ritual combat is the societal norm, that will ripple into law and family life whether you intend it to or not. So it's easy to see the importance of worldbuilding in these cases.

However, worldbuilding can mean the difference between adequate and great *nonfiction*.

A textbook may give you names and dates. A narrative history gives you atmosphere—economic pressure, political climate, social assumptions—so that decisions make sense within their time. A magazine article about whale migration might include the roll of the boat, the history of commercial whaling in the region, and the tourism industry that threatens it. Those details don't exist for decoration. They situate the reader.

In nonfiction, of course, you're not inventing the world. Rather, you're selecting which parts of reality to illuminate so the reader becomes immersed in it.

That's still worldbuilding.

## My Own Habit (and Occasional Surprise)

I'm a character-driven writer, which means I often set them loose in a sparsely imagined world and let them tell me what they see, hear, and know. I love the discovery, but sometimes, they run across something outside their experience, and I have to stop and think, halfway into the story, what this means for them and what clues they should have had beforehand.

Some writers prefer to map everything in advance, and can take years in worldbuilding before a character ever takes a step on the page.

Both approaches work, provided you eventually think through the consequences of what you've introduced—and you actually get to writing your story.

## Where We're Headed

In the chapters ahead, we'll look at a practical framework for thinking about your world so you don't overlook essential systems. We'll talk about ripple effects—how one change spreads outward to cause other changes. We'll cover how to research without drowning in it, and how to reveal what you know without turning your story into a lecture.

In every chapter, we'll consider how these principles apply whether you're inventing a new planet or writing about 1930s Detroit.

The goal isn't to produce elaborate encyclopedias. It's to create worlds that feel coherent enough that readers can relax inside them. Once that happens, they stop questioning the ground beneath the story.

They just walk on it.

CHAPTER ONE

# Put Your STAMP ON Your World

Every world has systems. Even the ones that look simple. Take, for example, a child playing in the backyard. That yard exists inside geography, weather, family rules, neighborhood politics, school hierarchies, economic realities, and whatever larger events are unfolding beyond the fence. You may never name all of those systems on the page, but they're there, shaping what can and cannot happen.

When thinking about worldbuilding, it's easy to focus on what's flashy—the magic, the spaceship, the murder weapon—and forget the infrastructure that makes those things plausible. The flashy part gets attention. The infrastructure keeps the story standing.

When I teach worldbuilding, I use a mnemonic to keep students (and myself) from overlooking something obvious. It's a practical way to make sure we haven't built a house and forgotten to check whether it has plumbing.

It's called STAMP ON. STAMP ON stands for:

Social

Technological

Animal

Military

Political

Origin

Natural

You don't need a master's thesis of research (or even a DnD manual's worth) in each category before you begin writing. And, of course, how much you think about each depends on the size of your story. Short stories need less preparation as a rule than a full series, for example.

Regardless, if you haven't at least glanced at each one, there's a good chance something structural is missing from your world.

Let's walk through them.

## Social

This is comprised of the social rules and norms we take for granted and which provide the texture of daily life.

Who holds authority? What does family look like? What's considered polite? What's scandalous? What assumptions do people grow up with that they don't even notice until it's pointed out to them? These questions shape your character and your adventure and can give the readers insight without explaining

Take the Shire in *The Hobbit* and *Lord of the Rings* by J.R.R. Tolkien. Tolkien gives us a delightful view of hobbit priorities: comfort, food, predictability, and a strong sense of community that even includes the relatives you don't like. So when Bilbo makes a difficult and unpopular decision to join the dwarves on an adventure, Tolkien doesn't have to tell us it was hard. We see the social expectations he's violating and just how foreign and scary the concept is even before he enters strange lands and faces danger.

When you create a believable society, readers will accept the most outlandish things.

Look at *The Hunger Games* by Suzanne Collins. Children are forced to kill each other in ritual combat, which is televised for the world to see. It's horrific and for most of us, inconceivable, yet Collins has crafted a society that accepts it. Everything from the indulgences of the Capitol's inhabitants to the way the districts regard each other creates a social scaffolding that makes the violence plausible inside the world.

In nonfiction, the same principle applies. One of the best books I've ever read is *The Girls Who Stepped Out of Line* by Major General Mari K. Eder. It's about women spies in WWII. The dangerous work these women did was impressive enough, but what made the book come alive was how they both defied and worked within the social conventions of the time. In fact, there were moments when the particular society's attitudes towards women saved their lives.

Social systems tell us what your characters believe is normal, and if you portray it well enough, the reader will also believe it's normal for the course of the story.

## Technological

Technology is not limited to gadgets and circuitry. It is the practical application of knowledge about nonhuman things that do work, whether mechanical or magical.

*Harry Potter* by J.K. Rolling is a great example of this because it has both the mundane and the magical worlds running in parallel, with only the occasional (and often hilarious) intersections between them, like the public toilets that take you to the Ministry of Magic. The result makes the magical world feel more whimsical and exciting, yet also more dangerous, as so many of the characters trust magic to make things alright. For example, imagine what would happen if a middle school assigned kids to clean the local lion's den for detention. But helping Hagrid in the Forbidden Forest is perfectly acceptable—don't worry, they'll have their wands.

## Animal

And speaking of Forbidden Forests, let's talk about the animals. Very often, this gets minimal treatment except for the specific creatures the humans need. But animals can be integral to the plot.

*Dune* by Frank Herbert doesn't work without the sandworms. They motivate the plot, define the ecology and the economy, not just of the planet but the entire empire. They're central to the religion and politics of the Fremen. Remove the worms and everything collapses.

This can also include any biological life, from *Harry Potter*'s car-wrecking Whomping Willow which seemed to have a mind of its own, to the alien virus in *The Andromeda Strain*.

Don't just include the ones that are integral to the story. Sometimes, they add color or humor. One of my favorite scenes in *The Incredibles* is when Dash Parr is running for his life through the jungle and runs straight into a swarm of gnats. He could have tripped for any reason, but the gnats not only provide a moment of humor in a tense situation but are also so relatable!

In nonfiction as well, animals can add color or be the entire purpose of the book or article. They can also provide an opportunity for metaphor or scene setting.

Ask yourself: What grows here? What hunts here? What gets eaten? What pollinates crops? What survives drought? What migrates?

## Military

This doesn't have to mean armored divisions or wartime maneuvers. For the purpose of this exercise, it refers to any officially-sanctioned, organized group used for enforcement and protection. That includes law enforcement, organized resistance, security forces, mercenaries, border patrol, even neighborhood watch groups.

Ask yourself: Who enforces order? How? With what authority?

In the Sherlock Holmes stories by Sir Arthur Conan Doyle, you have Scotland Yard, and Holmes and Watson often interact with them on a cordial, if adversarial basis. In my *DragonEye,*

*PI* series, Vern, a dragon detective with even more intelligence than Holmes but far less patience and fewer manners, has a much more adversarial relationship with the local police, but one with grows more cooperative over the series.

Even if you don't include the authorities in your novel, their effect will be there in how secure people feel. Contrast *Mad Max* by Geroge Miller and Byron Kennedy vs. *Divergent* by Veronica Roth. Both are post-apocalyptic worlds where survival as a species is tantamount. In *Mad Max*, there is no overarching governing authority with an organized enforcement, and the "military" is mostly rival gangs, so chaos reigns. In *Divergent*, there's an ultra-strong enforcement to maintain a rule of law that (much as we'd disagree with it) maintains a relatively peaceful society.

In nonfiction, think about the American West before established law enforcement. How different it is now. Suppose you're writing about the Capital Hill Autonomous Zone in Seattle, Washington—you can't without addressing "military" in terms of enforcing laws.

Where there is authority and a need to protect a group, territory, or possessions, someone carries it out.

## Political

Ask Google's AI to define politics, and it will tell you, "the process, art, and science of governing, making group decisions, and exercising power." Most dictionaries will limit this to government, but I agree more with the general approach.

Anyone who's served in the PTA or on a church board knows they can be political. A university department is political. Even a family with a domineering matriarch has its own kind of politics.

Sometimes, politics are the engine the runs the story, like in *A Game of Thrones* by George R.R. Martin or *Man in the High Castle* by Philip K. Dick. Other times, like in the *Valdemar* books by Mercedes Lackey, politics are a central underpinning, but not *the* story. Other times, politics provide a side plot or motivation. Fans of *Bridgerton* will mostly see the deep friendship between Queen Charlotte and Lady Danbury, but in Season Four, Lady Danbury makes it clear to Alice Mondrich that being a Lady-in-Waiting is a political advantage as well.

In real life, especially in modern society, politics affects everything from art to economics to people's mental health. And not just at the government level. There are plenty of trending videos on handling politics inside the office, from emails to confronting the boss. You may choose not to include politics in your work—for example, I don't include the local artist's rant about the current president in her interview. However, you need to consider how they shape the topic that you're writing about.

## Origin

How did your world come to be?

Not necessarily cosmologically, unless that matters. It's okay to start with a flat disk held by elephants on the back of a turtle if you can sell it. Rather, I mean historically.

In *Foundation* by Isaac Asimov, the predicted fall of a galactic empire shapes every strategic decision. That origin event creates momentum. The same for *Travelers,* although the apocalypse has already happened and Travelers are sent back in time to try to prevent it.

In my *DragonEye, PI* series, the origin is not the creation of the Faerie and Mundane worlds, but the accident that connects them through the Gap.

None of these is the actual origin of the world itself, but the origin of the world for the book: the conflict, the tension, the inciting incident for the book-universe that will lay the foundation for everything contained in it.

If you write nonfiction, you have it both easier and harder, because too often, you can't point to one thing and say, "That's how it started." The Great Depression was a combination of factors from war to the weather. Looked at in isolation, the assassination of Prince Ferdinand should not have started worldwide war.

However, like with fiction, you have the freedom to pick the aspects that apply most to your story. Just be sure you are aware of the others. And of course, length and subject dictate how much attention you give origin. A book on current taxation code in the U.S. is going to need a lot more origin story than a how-to article on payroll taxes.

## Natural

This includes anything non-life that is part of the ecosystem: geography, climate, seasons, even natural disasters.

How does geography affect your world? A. Trae McMaken's *The Dwarves of Ice-Cloak* books make great use of geography. It's central to how the main character finds and builds his kingdom and influences everything that threatens it from then on, from harsh winters to ambush points for pushing back invading forces.

Say you want to build a system with two moons. That doesn't just make an interesting night sky. It affects tides, the seasons (a season of dark when neither moon is visible). It might even affect religion. For a great example of this, check out Colleen Drippé's *Gelen*.

In nonfiction, geography shapes industry, politics, even social mores. Civilizations spring up where there's water and weather for growing things. People living in the tropics may define modesty differently. Weather events like hurricanes can reshape entire cities culturally as well as physically.

Nature exerts pressure whether acknowledged or not.

## Using STAMP ON Without Turning It Into Homework

You've got enough to do crafting your story. Don't use STAMP ON as an academic exercise. Instead, use it to check that the world you've imagined can stand up under its own weight, or if you've missed something that can add additional depth to your story or prose.

You may find that one category barely matters for your story. A small-town cozy mystery might not require a detailed examination of the natural ecosystem, but it probably requires a clear social fabric and local political dynamics. A regency romance may not need political commentary, but it must understand the natural and technological realities of the era. An article about the use of AI may not need an examination of nature—unless, of course, it's talking about the effect of AI on the environment.

The goal is not completeness for its own sake. It's about understanding the nuances of your world well enough that your character—and your reader—can walk in it.

Whether you're inventing a desert planet or reconstructing 1930s Detroit, the question remains the same: Have you considered the systems that make this place function?

If not, you may still tell a good story, but the world will feel lighter than it needs to.

Next chapter, we'll talk about how to build your world through one simple question:

*What if?*

## Reflection Questions

- Which part of STAMP ON comes most naturally to you?
- Which one do you usually ignore?
- If someone were to ask you the root cause of your world, could you answer specifically?
- Are your characters reacting inside a functioning system, or are they operating in a vacuum?
- In nonfiction: Are you presenting events, or are you presenting events within their social, political, technological, and natural context?

## Exercise: The STAMP Snapshot

Using STAMP ON, jot down three to five quick notes about your current project's world for each letter. Just write what you know, but if a question comes up, note it elsewhere.

For example:

- **Social:** tight-knit rural community; strong church presence; gossip spreads fast
- **Technological:** limited cell service; farming equipment; no hospital in town
- **Natural:** harsh winters; isolated roads; river floods every spring

If you can't come up with three notes for a category, that's useful information. Ask yourself if you need to know more, or if it's sufficient for the purposes of your story.

CHAPTER TWO

# Asking "What If?"

Last chapter, we looked at the systems that make up a world. STAMP ON helps you notice what exists: the social fabric, the technology, the animals and ecology, the military structures, the political power, the origin story, the natural environment.

If you've applied this to your own world, you probably identified things you don't know. If you're just started, then you have a framework for getting started.

You may be thinking the next step is to jump into research. I'm going to ask you to hold off a little. We'll cover research in later chapters, but first, I want to talk about what all those facts mean. I believe that helps you focus your research—and know when the time has come to stop scrolling Google links and start writing.

So, let's talk about cause and effect and the ripples one part of worldbuilding can cause to the rest of your world.

After all, a convincing world doesn't just mean a list of elements artfully placed in a story or article. Rather, it becomes real when you understand and demonstrate how they work together—and how they react to change.

The simplest way to begin that process is with a question you've probably been asking since childhood:

*What if?*

- What if the gravity is heavier?
- What if magic is real?
- What if zombies are an international problem?
- What if the moon behaves differently?

The question itself is easy. The discipline comes in refusing to stop at the first answer.

## Ripple Thinking and the Jovian Problem

If you alter the mineral content of a world, you might lower its gravity; lower the gravity too much and you lose atmosphere. Lose enough atmosphere and more radiation strikes your planet. More radiation striking the planet means…

That's ripple thinking. That takes your story from "basically humans just elsewhere" to a truly unique world.

Remember how I told you that an author describing a Jovian only as short and strong bothered me? When I got the chance to write a story on the giant planet, I decided to go further.

I started with "What if we genetically engineered ourselves to live inside the gas giant? What would that look like? How would they move? How would they breathe?"

Next, I started asking myself other questions in STAMP ON: What would the society look like? What if they used animal DNA in the process? (Animal) What if a storm was coming to the settlement to rival the Red Spot? (Nature) What if the genetic engineers couldn't decide on one type of mutation? (Politics)"

In the end, I wrote "Jovian Heat," a noir mystery about a woman detective investigating a paternity case where the father died before the child was conceived. She's investigating as the town is evacuating in anticipation of a hundred-year storm—and she's dealing with all the physical and emotional challenges of being in heat.

The characters are still human in their joys and sorrows, devotions and vices, but they are also vibrantly alien as befits the harshly alien landscape of a gas giant.

That is the difference between a decorative detail and a functioning world.

## How Things Work Together

It's not enough to know a rule; you must understand how that rule interacts with others. This in turn causes a chain of thinking.

- How does physics affect geology?
- How does geology affect the growth of civilization?
- How does civilization shape culture?

Those questions move you from premise to plausibility. Let's look at something somewhat less scientific.

I wrote a book called *Neeta Lyffe, Zombie Exterminator*. It takes place in the 2040s (I wrote it in 2009) and the premise was simple: The zombie apocalypse happened, but we handled it intelligently, like we would any other outbreak of disease. From there, the ripples moved outward.

Governments enacted quick laws to isolate and remove the infected. Laws like requiring that all dead must have their spines severed before burial helped prevent reanimation. That reduced the outbreak so much that zombies became the exception rather than the rule. Hence, a new specialization—exterminators who also take out the undead.

But zombieism has changed everything from entertainment to conspiracy theories. Waring countries ally to battle the undead rising from the battlefield. A movement rises of people insisting zombies have rights—never mind that they'll eat you. Scientific research into cures and repellents becomes a major industry.

Zombieism is not the whole world. It is the stone thrown into the pond, and the ripples create a whole new world.

## The Technology That Changed the World

Zombies are fun and all, but what about real life? There's a story I heard about a college history professor asking what single invention changed the entire world. While some people suggested steam engines or cell phones, one person gave the answer he'd hoped for: the invention of the stirrup.

Yep, the stirrup, that little piece of metal on a saddle where you can stuff your feet. It's innocuous, until you look at the ripples:

- Stirrups gave more stability.
- More stability meant warriors on horseback could shoot arrows more accurately, but even more, they could use a lance without being knocked off the horse.
- A stronger cavalry meant military advantage, but horses, armor, etc. were

expensive. To encourage mounted warriors to stay loyal, Lords started granting land. This led to European feudalism.

- With knights now owning land, they developed a class identity. This led to codes of chivalry and changes in court culture. Knights become heroes and romantic figures in literature.
- Architecture changes to accommodate horses and to withstand cavalry-based warfare.
- Industries around knights, like saddle-makers and armorers, grow. Agriculture favors pastureland. Blacksmithing advances.
- Meanwhile, nomadic tribes now have more martial capability.

All this from a little curve of metal on a strap of leather.

## Tracking the Ripples in Fiction

These examples may feel pretty easy when reading them after-the-fact. The books are written, history has happened. But how do you use "What if" in a new world without getting stuck or overwhelmed?

Start with the world you know. That doesn't have to mean modern Earth, just whatever you know about the world of your story. Then pick the most important element. In a way, that is your "origin" from STAMP ON. Now run it through the rest of the letters. Ask yourself:

- What if this had happened on Earth or to a culture I know (such as if you're basing off a fairy-tale land).
- What is the worst thing this element can do to my world? What's the best? What's the funniest? What's the most tragic?
- How does this shape my character and those around them?

Some of these questions you might not be able to answer right away. Those will take research or they may answer themselves as you write.

You can also use these questions in the editing process by looking to see if you answered them or revealed these changes. It could point to places where you might deepen your world. It may even point to the next book in the series!

## Nonfiction: Tracing Real Ripples

Nonfiction worldbuilding is the disciplined tracing of real consequences.

Sometimes, the "what if" has already occurred. Many years ago, I read a *National Geographic* article on blue whales. It was beautifully done as the best *National Geographic* articles are, both factual and immersive. While it was about whale migration, the writer also included tactile details like the motion of the boat he was on, the history of whale hunting, the growth of tourism in Costa Rica, and even a boating accident that injured a whale.

But why include tourism in a whale article?

Because tourism affected the whales' habitat; specifically, their spawning area. The boating incident added a strong emotional punch as well as illustrated the danger.

Those are ripple effects in the real world.

When tracing ripples in nonfiction, keep an eye on long-term influences and real-world examples.

Other times, the "What if" leads to serious discussion and calls to action. *In the Future of Feeling* by Kaitlin Ugolik Phillips begins with the premise, "What if we are losing our empathy?" and then addresses not only what this means to society, mental health, and politics, but also how technology both harms and can help with empathy.

## Where Writers Stop Too Soon

Most shallow worldbuilding fails not because the writer lacked imagination, but because the writer stopped after the first visible change.

- Heavy gravity creates stronger people.
- Magic becomes convenient solutions.
- Zombies become an unstoppable threat.

But systems resist imbalance. People adapt. Institutions reorganize. Markets exploit. And the result is a strange new world that's fun to write about.

You do not need to chase every ripple to infinity. You do need to follow them far enough that the world feels reactive instead of static. Then your characters will not just perform in it, but actually live.

"What if" is not just a powerful tool for plot development, but for worldbuilding. It helps you see the ripples just one change can make.

In the next chapter, we will talk about what happens when you establish rules and then forget to obey them.

## Reflection

Consider one central change in your current project.

- What is the initial what if?
- What immediate consequence follows?
- What secondary consequence emerges from that?
- Who benefits from this change?
- Who is threatened by it?
- What belief or practice shifts because of it?

If you are writing nonfiction, substitute a real development—industrialization, a new law, a migration, a technological innovation—and ask the same questions.

Where consequences accumulate, story grows.

## Exercise: Follow the Ripples

Choose one foundational element in your work—invented or historical.

- Write a brief chain of consequences:
- What if this exists?
- What changes immediately?
- What changes because of that?
- How do people adapt?
- What tension results?

Keep it under a page. This is not exposition for your manuscript. It is scaffolding for your understanding.

When the elements of your world begin to affect one another, the setting gains weight. And when the setting gains weight, characters can lean against it—or be crushed by it.

CHAPTER THREE

# Internal Logic: The World Must Obey Itself

By now, you've identified the systems in your world (STAMP ON), and you've learned how asking "What if" can disturb a world or build it higher.

The next thing we're going to discuss before we move on to the actual task of worldbuilding is keeping an internal logic. That means it must obey its own laws, whether it's the law of variable gravity, or the laws of nature that drive the turtle who holds your world to find a mate.

(Yep, Pratchett went there in *The Light Fantastic*.)

Readers will accept almost anything—an uploaded human mind who explores the universe by cloning himself, fish people on Jupiter, zombie exterminators, mating space turtles... It's all up for grabs provided *the world behaves consistently*.

That's where the key is. Readers expect the world to have some kind of logic. Even the movie *Everything Everywhere All At Once*, which is an insane roller coaster of quantum probabilities, has its own twisted system of operation. That's what makes it brilliant and loved by fans.

Lose that, whether because of lazy writing or because it no longer fits your plot, and you will annoy your reader at best and lose him at worse—unless you think "worse" is being ruthlessly panned on the Internet.

(Sigh. I should live to be so popular.)

## When Physics Is Flexible (But Not Forgetful)

We've talked about ripple effects. If you alter the mineral content of a planet, you alter gravity which affects atmosphere, etcetera. Those are ripple effects. Internal logic is what prevents you from ignoring them once established.

This applies to the details of your story. If you have a planet of people who look and move like fishes, they aren't going to be sitting on a standard couch or eating off china.

But it's more than that. Some things need rules to make sense. Magic is a prime example. I'm not saying you need a DnD-level set of rules for every spell or that you need to explain all the rules in your book. It's more about execution.

If a spell works one way in one scene and another way later because the plot requires it, the reader senses manipulation. Stable rules create tension. Unstable rules dissolve it.

In *The Lord of the Rings* by J.R.R. Tolkien, magic is rarely explained in technical terms, yet it operates within consistent moral and metaphysical boundaries. The Ring corrupts, always; it does not occasionally purify because it would be convenient. Purer people like Samwise can resist, but that doesn't change its nature. The consistency of that corruption is what gives it weight.

The rules do not have to be scientific. They do have to be dependable.

## Culture Is a System, Not a Costume

Internal logic applies just as strongly to social and religious systems as it does to physics.

Long ago—during the first Iraqi war, I think—I beta read a book about an American soldier who was captured. In one scene, the author made a big deal about a senior officer officially excusing guards from prayer so they could guard the prisoner who they had stored in a tent.

He was trying to show he understood how important prayer was, but he lost me because he didn't think about how this would work in a combat situation. As a result, he turned the soldiers into stereotypes.

If you do not understand how the practice works, you risk writing something that may sound plausible but is incorrect, even if for a specific situation.

Readers who know the culture will recognize the error immediately. (In this case, I knew from my own military experience rather than from being a Muslim.)

Similarly, if you write a plucky feminist in medieval Scotland who moves freely without resistance, you have altered more than a personality trait. You've introduced an anachronism without a consequence—or you've altered the surrounding society. Either the culture is different in foundational ways, or your character will encounter friction.

Either choice is fine, but be aware that it is a choice. You don't get to have both unless you are willing to alienate readers who care about continuity.

## Use Technology to Its Fullest

I love *Star Trek*. I grew up watching it during dinner. My husband and I met because of *Star*

*Trek*. But it's not the best for consistent worldbuilding or use of technology.

Take phasers for example. Phasers have a stun setting. A *stun* setting. Zap someone, and they'll wake up with a headache, but that's about it. And yet how many times does someone hesitate to shoot for some reason—they have a hostage, it's a possessed crewman—and as a result the ship is in even greater danger later?

It's not just *Star Trek*—any sci fi with a stunner magically forgets that using it won't kill the person, so they hesitate.

To me, that's sloppy worldbuilding. Of course in our everyday world, good guys don't just shoot someone. Even tasing has consequences. But in space, with the ship in danger, where the stun setting is a widely accepted technology with known minimal consequences? For a competent crewman, let alone a security officer, it should be a no-brainer.

My husband and I shout at the TV: *Shoot them! Headaches Save Lives*. When I started writing *Star Trek* parody, the first thing I did was make sure the chief of security told his teams, "Stun first; work it out with the captain later."

*Headaches Save Lives!* is the motto of the HMB Impulsive Security team.

Checkov—Anton, not Ensign Pavel—said, "If in the first act you have hung a pistol on the wall, then in the following one it should be fired." I offer a corollary: *If in your world you have a technology, then that technology should be used to its logical fullest.*

## Tone Does Not Replace Structure

Comedy and satire can stretch reality, but they do not escape it.

In *Hitchhiker's Guide to the Galaxy*, Douglas Adams has a ship run by an infinite improbability drive. Here's how he explains its origin:

> The principle of generating small amounts of finite improbability by simply hooking up the logic circuits...were of course well understood—and such generators were often used...
>
> ...(after) the perpetual failure (physicists) encountered in trying to construct a machine which could generate the infinite improbability field...they grumpily

> announced that such a machine was virtually impossible.
>
> Then, one day, a student…found himself reasoning this way:
>
> If…such a machine is a virtual impossibility, then it must logically be a *finite* improbability. So all I have to do in order to make one is to work out exactly how improbable it is, feed that figure into the machine, give it a cup of really hot tea…and turn it on!
>
> He did this and was rather startled to discover that he had managed to create the long-sought-after golden Infinite Improbability generator out of thin air.
>
> *Hitchhikers Guide to the Galaxy* by Douglas Adams (1979: Pocket Books), pgs. 85-86

I laugh every time I read this, and yet, there is a twisted logic that makes me think, "Maybe…" That's because he set the rules—anything improbable can be created if the exact improbability is fed into the machine (with strong tea), then used it to its logical conclusion.

Even the most whimsical worlds must obey their own premises. Otherwise, the reader's laughter turns into confusion.

## Nonfiction: Coherence, Context, Correctness

Internal logic matters just as much in nonfiction. Most of the time, this will be obvious, since you are familiar with the reality you're writing about, but tone can be an issue. If you are painting something as bad or wrong and without warning say it had advantages, you need to be ready to qualify that statement.

One thing that is vital is checking your facts. If your target audience knows the material well and you get it wrong, they will assume laziness or bias. Either way, you lost them as a future reader.

The same goes for interpretation. If you misrepresent how a legal process works or how a religious practice functions, you lose trust at best. If you misrepresent a person or business, you could face libel, even if you are using them for detail and worldbuilding color.

Consistency in nonfiction is not about obeying invented rules; it is about accurately reflecting real systems.

## Breaking the Rule on Purpose

There are times when you will bend or break a rule deliberately.

You may promote the cadet in extraordinary circumstances. (Cadet to Captain Kirk, anyone?) You may design a medieval society with radically different gender norms. You may allow magic to be unstable.

The issue isn't whether you can break the rule, but whether the world absorbs that break coherently.

- What structural change accompanies the exception?
- What consequence follows?
- What new tension emerges?

A rule broken without adjustment feels convenient.

Internal logic isn't always easy, especially when it interferes with plot convenience, but it not only grounds the reader but can add a new dramatic tension to the story or force you to find creative ways around an issue—even if that means a different way to get the ship in trouble because Ensign Gel stunned the bad guy.

In the next chapter, we will look at different ways writers construct their worlds in the first place, from borrowing frameworks to letting characters drag the setting into existence.

## Reflection Questions

- What physical rule governs your world (gravity, technology limits, environmental conditions)? Have you applied it consistently?
- What social norm shapes behavior (gender roles, religious practice, class hierarchy)? Where do we see it reinforced?
- What institutional structure exists (military chain of command, corporate hierarchy, political system)? Does it function the same way in every scene?
- Are your characters using technology the way someone of their world should? If not, are there believable reasons they can't or won't?
- In nonfiction: What contextual factor have you introduced (economic pressure, geography, technology)? Does it continue to shape events throughout your narrative? Do you stay consistent?

## Exercise: The Consistency Audit

Choose one established rule or system in your world. Write a short audit addressing:

- Where is this rule first established?
- What scenes depend on it?
- What scenes might contradict it?
- What would realistically happen if someone violated it?
- Have you shown that consequence?

If you are writing nonfiction, choose one contextual factor—economic policy, cultural practice, technological limitation—and trace whether it consistently influences your narrative.

Don't feel the need to add exposition to explain anything. This exercise is for recognizing and removing contradiction.

CHAPTER FOUR

# Building Your World

The fun begins! Research? No, that's next chapter. First, let's talk practical ways to build your world.

We've looked at structure (STAMP ON), ripple effects ("What if?"), and internal logic. Those chapters assume that you have at least the start of a world to examine. (Although "What if" also works for creating a world from scratch, as we saw with *Jovian Heat*.)

Now we're going to look at some ways a world comes into being in the first place.

Some writers begin with a place—a planet, a mountainside, a magical academy. Others begin with a political system, a theological premise, or a quirk of physics. Many begin with a character and discover, somewhat to their surprise, that the world expands to accommodate that character's needs.

Sometimes, though, you may only start with an idea, a plot point, and you need a world. Or your starting point has only provided so much information, even with "what if" to push you on.

I'm going to share four ways I and others have built worlds: borrowing and reshaping, analogy and adaptation, character-driven construction, and organic growth over time.

## The Stolen World: Parody, Adaptation, and Inspired Frameworks

Sometimes a world begins because you love another one.

You want to play with starships or wizards or a specific tone of space opera. So, you borrow a shape, then mold it to your vision.

My series *Space Traipse: Hold My Beer* began as a playful mash-up of *Star Trek* and a Tumblr post about how humans rule the galaxy because they are insanely yet successfully reckless. I wanted a familiar structure where I could parody science fiction tropes in a loving way (like the stun setting—Headaches Save Lives!)

If you look, you can see some of the parallels to Starfleet and the aliens, the starship and replicators, but then I used humor and "What if" to make it something that stands on its own. You don't have to be a Star Trek fan.

Let's take transporters, for example—or, in my world, *teleporters* so Paramount doesn't sue me. It's long surmised in Star Trek folklore that a transporter essentially destroys you on a quantum level and sends the information to build a new you on the other side. In other words, you're killed. That's pretty heavy, but other than some griping, everyone goes with it.

In *Space Traipse*, however, it's sprouted a whole new culture—the telegoths, teleporter operators who embrace the dark side of their job with almost religious fanaticism. This means Chief Dour dresses in black robes during tense missions, calls the console his "Mistress," and always has a proclamation of death and rebirth that the rest of the crew shrug off.

That kind of building requires awareness. If readers recognize the source material, they bring expectations with them. You can meet those expectations, subvert them, or redirect them, but you cannot pretend they do not exist.

Consider *West Side Story*. Really, it's *Romeo and Juliet* in mid-twentieth-century New York gang culture. The plot is virtually the same, as is the conflict, but the change in time and place changes everything. Instead of Renaissance family politics, you have gang rivalry, along with light racism. In all, it makes a familiar story feel brand new because the adaptation is structural, not cosmetic.

Borrowing works when you ask STAMP ON questions of the adopted framework. What changes socially? What changes politically? What natural or technological conditions differ? The more deliberately you answer those questions, the more distinct your world becomes.

Nonfiction naturally uses this method. After all, you are pulling from the world for your article or book. You simply choose what aspects you need and how you express them.

Borrowing can be a fast and easy way to worldbuild, but it's vital that you don't just grab a world and paste it into your story. In fiction, you must adapt it to make it yours. In nonfiction, you have to be sure you use what supports the story.

## Analogous Worlds: Adapting Real Cultures

Another common method is to take part of an existing culture and adapt it.

You might pattern an army after ancient Rome, pull from Chinese fairy tales to populate your world with creatures, or borrow from cryptoculture to build your galactic economic system. The goal is not to replicate the thing you borrow but to adapt its structure to suit your world.

When you do this well, you go beyond the surface details and explore backgrounds, first causes, motivations, power structures, and more.

In STAMP ON terms, analogy requires you to ask questions like:

- What social norms am I importing?
- What technological level supports this system?
- What political assumptions travel with them?
- What natural environment shaped it originally, and does that environment still exist here?

The television series *Firefly* puts the American frontier into outer space. The aesthetic is familiar—they even have horses and guns—but the technology, governance, and economic imperatives reshape it. Then to make it even more interesting, they throw in a generous amount of Chinese language, costume, and culture. The show works because it does not simply put cowboy hats on starships; it adapts frontier economics and social isolation into interplanetary form.

Worldbuilding in nonfiction is a good way to come up with analogies. For example, you might compare the dot-com era to the California gold rush. They both shared optimism and risk, occasional great successes and spectacular failures. When doing something like this, just be sure your parallels are truly parallel. Also, be sure your audience knows the "world" you are pulling from.

If you borrow cultural patterns, you must also respect internal logic. Either you must carry it over, or you need to adapt it. Regardless, it must fit with the overall structure of your world.

## Analogous Creatures: Adapting Real Science

When looking for creatures to occupy your world, there are plenty of myths and fables to pull from, but some of the most fascinating creatures can be created from looking at the ones occupying our world right now.

There are an estimated 1.2 to 2 million species that have been catalogued, from aphids to zebras, and each has its own unique physical characteristics, strengths and weaknesses, and even cultures. Many a successful writer has pulled from Earth-born species to create their alien ones. *Star Trek* has some well-known examples. It has several cat like species, including the Kzinti, a warlike cat species they borrowed from Larry Niven's *Known Space* series, and when the Gorn needed a serious glow-up, they turned to insects to create a hive-mind like bees and the need to lay eggs in another species, like wasps. And of course, who doesn't love the sapient dolphins that man Cetacean Ops in *Lower Decks*?

You don't have to use one creature—sometimes pulling from multiple species to create a chimera of an alien gives you a unique twist. Other times, you may want to think, "what species would best survive on my world?" and evolve them up to sapience.

## The Character-Driven World

Not every world begins with a system. Sometimes it begins with a person.

Let's look at my *DragonEye, PI* series (because I know it best.) I wrote Vern, my dragon detective and MC, for a single short story. However, I loved him so much—and others did, too—that he needed more stories. That meant more world for him to move through—more people to encounter, organizations to butt heads with, magic and technology to go wrong and give him headaches.

Soon I had a complex world of mages and magical creatures, regular humans from live action role players to the local National Guard, superspies, superheroes... There's even an amusement park/commercial center-turned movie production studio—with hobgoblins as the caretakers! Every story brings something new, and I scramble to keep track of it all. (We'll talk about that in the Story Bible chapter.)

If you are a character-driven writer, this may be the most natural way to grow your world, but it's not without its pitfalls. Everything is a surprise, and occasionally something happens that seems to contradict the past.

Thus, character-driven worlds sometimes require revision. As you learn more about the setting, earlier scenes may need adjustment. The challenge is in maintaining consistency and internal logic as you expand.

I'll be honest, the bigger the series, the harder it is. Any *Star Trek* fan can tell you how the most recent shows are being lambasted for missing key elements of the established canon.

I ran into this myself as I got more determined to write a large story arc with Vern. That meant going back and making sure the world and he were coherent. I made the radical decision in 2020 to reboot the entire series and am retconning the early books and stories.

Just because the character in nonfiction isn't imaginary doesn't mean they don't build a world, too. A memoirist may begin with a personal memory and branch into the landscape, society, economics, or religious influences that shape the experience.

The same for history. Notice how the world of politics, war, women's liberation, and early flight are all seen as Jackie Cochran and Elanor Roosevelt move through them.

> The WASP program itself was born from another dream. Jackie Cochran had been a

famous pilot in the 1930s, winning air races and competing against the likes of Amelia Earhard. In 1939, she wrote a letter to First Lady Elanor Roosevelt, presenting her case for making women pilots eligible for military service.

Elanor Roosevelt had taken flying lessons herself, and she immediately grasped the significance of Jackie's proposal. The First Lady use her platform to become an outspoken supporter of the WASP. She wrote in her newspaper column, My Day, "This is not a time when women should be patient. We are in war and we need to fight with all our ability and every weapon possible..."

*The Girls Who Stepped Out of Line* by Major General Mari K. Eder (2022: Sourcebooks) pg. 264

Character-first does not eliminate structure. It reveals structure incrementally.

## The World That Grows as You Write

Related to character-driven building is the world that expands over time.

You begin with a premise and a few assumptions. As the narrative continues—especially in a series—you realize that neighboring regions, political alliances, or theological differences now matter. What was once a passing reference becomes a necessary structure.

This happened to me in my *Madness of Kanaan* series. I had two warring worlds—Barin and Kanaan. I only ever intended Barin to be the bad guys in the war. But as the two cultures prepared for war, I started realizing I needed better motivation than "They want to colonize." I also needed a better explanation why a spacefaring world would come, attack, and leave without establishing strongholds and regular supply runs.

That led me to discover a truly barren world on the brink of destruction, a subterranean people desperate for a new home, and a half-crazed alien—a traitor to Kanaan—whom they worshiped with fanatical devotion.

Another great example is Terry Pratchett's Discworld, which grew to include new races, witches as well as wizards, even a broken-down post office in need of a shyster to revive it. Already fanciful of itself, books came out about the myths like the Hogfather and a new take on the Tooth Fairy.

Like when your character grows your world, you're better off if you keep track of what's invented. Everything new needs to fit in the old rules—or the rules must adapt logically. You can use STAMP ON to check expansion for coherence.

In nonfiction, you can see this kind of worldbuilding in long investigative projects. A journalist may begin with a single event and discover connections to regulatory frameworks, historical precedents, and economic incentives. Or someone writing a self-help might find precedents in past studies, use myths and archetypes to enlighten, or veer into the economics of the problem they're trying to solve. As research deepens, the world widens.

Growth is natural and a lot of fun. The challenge is to keep those discoveries in check so that you maintain a coherent world.

In the next chapter, we will turn to research, with tips for finding the information to build your world—and also some suggestions to prevent research from becoming the world itself.

## Reflection Questions

Consider your current project and ask:

- Which method are you using most heavily—borrowing, analogy, character-driven development, or organic growth?
- If you are borrowing or adapting, what structural elements have you changed beyond aesthetics?
- If your world is character-driven, where has the character revealed gaps in your setting?
- If the world is expanding over time, are you tracking continuity?
- In nonfiction, are you building from an individual story outward, or from systemic context inward?

## Exercise: Identify Your Build Pattern

Write a brief paragraph describing how you started building your world.

Then list:

- One strength of that method.
- One weakness or blind spot.
- One STAMP ON category you may have underdeveloped because of your chosen approach.

For example, if you began with a character, you may have rich social detail but thin geopolitical structure. If you began with a borrowed framework, you may have aesthetic clarity but unexamined economic consequences.

Finally, choose one underdeveloped area and sketch three notes to strengthen it.

CHAPTER FIVE

# Making Research Work for Your World

Now, we're ready for research!

You may have already been thinking and maybe even looking up some answers to questions, so why are we halfway into the book before we start taking research seriously?

I've personally known many would-be authors who never get to their book or take months to write a single chapter because they are having so much fun with the research. You've probably seen the memes: A writer writes, "Veronica sat at her desk," then stops to spend three hours studying Victorian furniture making, medieval wood joinery, what lumber was used in Scotland in the era... and ends up saying, "the oak desk." The only thing worse is spending all that time researching the desk and never having your heroine sit at it!

By the time you reach research, you should already know what kind of world you are building. STAMP ON has helped you identify systems. "What if?" has shown you how they ripple. Internal logic has reminded you to keep your rules straight. Research exists to support those structures, not replace them.

It is possible to research endlessly and still not build a world. It is also possible to invent confidently and discover later that you misunderstood something fundamental. In fact, it's possible that this will happen even with all your research, especially if you are discovering the world as you go. The goal is not to become an expert in every field you touch. The goal is to know enough that your world behaves believably.

Naturally, you'll turn up really cool things in your research that will give your world sparkle. One of my favorite things about romance author Maddie Evans is how she brings in so many fun facts about the everyday world her characters live in—marathon running or knitting, or the right kind of knives for cutting different ingredients. But above all, your research needs to support the characters and the plot—otherwise, it's an encyclopedia hidden in a story.

Research is not about accumulating trivia. It is about understanding systems deeply enough that whatever you choose feels natural. That enhances the reader's experience.

## Sources: Where to Look

Research has become easier than ever because there are so many sources and we have such easy access.

The most obvious source is books, but not all books are equally useful. Dense academic texts may provide depth but get you so caught in the details you never get to how it applies to your character. When evaluating a book, look for detail and practicality—do you need to understand the equations for quantum entanglement, or do you just need to get the gist of the concept?

One thing I recommend is starting with children's books. My thirdborn loved animals and machines and had the best books as a child. I still have David Maccaulay's *Built To Last*, which talks about how castles, cathedrals, and mosques were built. In addition to excellent information on everything from building materials and definition of parts of the buildings, he has some lovely worldbuilding, too.

Children's books like this tend to be concise, structured, and written to explain systems clearly. If you are trying to understand geology, feudal structures, or the basics of Catholicism, a well-written middle-grade text can supply the most common answers, and if you need to go deeper, you have a foundation to build on.

Experts are another strong resource. It can be hard to make yourself reach out to a stranger. I know I always feel like I'm imposing, but remember that if they don't have time, they'll tell you (or ghost you). And those that do respond are usually eager to help.

I've had the best conversations with experts at all levels of worldbuilding. For *Madness of Kanaan*, I knew I wanted a reason for the worlds to not be able to fight each other all the time. My astronomy professor helped me develop a system of worlds whose orbits intersected twice a "year," which marked the time for invasion and retreat. It dictated the plot of three books.

When I wrote "Antivenom," I consulted a snake venom expert for real-world experience in treating victims of snake bites. And when I needed to know more about how California exterminators got their licenses, I called someone in the local licensing division. He was a little confused that my exterminator took out zombies, but his information made for a terrific chapter.

Sometimes, too, I'll rely on an expert to make sure I'm using or interpreting the facts correctly. I'd learned about neurolinguistic programming from a book and weekend college webinar, but I asked an actual practitioner to make sure my character was using it correctly and not just how I thought sounded cool.

That kind of consultation does more than confirm facts; it reveals nuance. It prevents you from relying on stereotypes or cinematic assumptions.

Naturally, the go-to nowadays is Google or some other search engine or even AI. I've personally asked ChatGPT for examples to use in this book. The thing to remember, though, is that search engines, and especially AI, don't always turn up the most correct information. (Try looking up "Flat Earth," and you'll find tons of sources that can sound convincing.) So when you use the internet in whatever capacity, ask for sources and check them directly and trust your instincts if something sounds off.

## Questions: What to Ask

Research has become harder than ever because there are so many sources and we have such easy access.

It becomes manageable when you begin with specific questions and goals. STAMP ON can provide a structure for those questions, and you may have several that spring from your "What if" or the basics of your plot. You can also brainstorm questions based on the quirks of your world as you already know it.

Let's go back to my story *Jovian Heat* as an example. I started with some basic facts about Jupiter and the fact that I wanted a noir detective as my MC. Well, most noir detective stories have alcohol as a plot point or trope. What would be the equivalent inside Jupiter? That led me to read up on atmospheric gasses—but just enough to learn that oxygen isn't a gas there. My characters wouldn't breathe it. Couldn't breathe it? So what if it affected them like alcohol? But they would breathe hydrogen, which means a dangerous combination if they have too much.

I didn't get into the math or what processes would happen to make my genetically engineered Jovian get a buzz, I merely used these facts to introduce a bit of color as she uses a mister to relax after a long day—and when she stops a man from being murdered by oxygen asphyxiation.

That process of using questions for targeted research prevents you from going down a rabbit hole. (Usually—results vary.) Instead of reading everything about medieval trade, you investigate the specific aspects that affect your character's livelihood.

## Research in Nonfiction

In fiction, if you get your research wrong, chances are the reader will forgive you or may even think you did it on purpose. Larry Correia tells the story of how he'd written about a helicopter (a Blackhawk, I believe) hovering over a navy ship so the team could jump to the deck and take out monsters. He's got a lot of military readers, and some noted that the particular helicopter he described could not hover that way. Another reader chimed in, "Skippy the orc was piloting. He probably used magic."

In nonfiction, research is the backbone of credibility, so it's vitally important that you be accurate.

You also need to limit what you share to the needs of your audience. If you are writing an economics book, for example, you may still include lively practical examples of the concepts, but you'll give more attention to definitions, deep dive examinations, even mathematical equations. If you're writing for the general audience, you'll stick with the examples and concise explanations of what they mean. In that case, your level of research does not have to be at a doctorate level.

Let's look at an example. This is from a PDF of *PH4401: Quantum Mechanics III* by Y.D. Chong at the University of Singapore:

> Suppose we have two particles labeled A and B. If each individual particle is treated as a quantum system, the postulates of quantum mechanics require that its state be described by a vector in a Hilbert space. Let HA and HB denote the respective single-particle Hilbert spaces. Then the Hilbert space for the combined system of two particles is H = HA ⊗ HB. (3.1) The

> symbol ⊗ refers to a tensor product, a mathematical operation that combines two Hilbert spaces to form another Hilbert space. It is most easily understood in terms of explicit basis vectors...
>
> *PH4401: Quantum Mechanics* III by Y.D. Chong (University of Singapore), pg. 37

Not a lot of worldbuilding, but the point is approach—technical, mathematical. Now, here's Space.com's explanation of the same concept:

> Quantum entanglement occurs when two subatomic particles become linked in such a way that their properties remain connected, no matter how far apart they are. A change to one particle seems to instantaneously influence the other, even if they are separated by billions of light-years.
>
> "What is quantum entanglement? The physics of 'spooky action at a distance' explained" by Daisy Dobrijevic, Jesse Emspak, and Kimberly Hickok Space.com (October 8, 2025)

See *how* they got right to the gist and explained it in simpler terms without the mathematics? The article doesn't even mention Hilbert spaces because it wasn't necessary for the reader's understanding.

That's the task of the nonfiction writer—to pull from the research to give the information their reader needs. As a result, their goal resembles the novelist's: understand enough to choose the details wisely.

## Nonfiction Follows Similar Processes

Nonfiction writers face the same challenge. A journalist writing about the restaurant industry must decide which details clarify hierarchy and which merely decorate the scene. Check out this example from *Built to Last*:

> Work continued until November, when colder temperatures threatened to crack the wet mortar. After protecting the tops of the unfinished walls with a covering of straw and dung, many of the workers returned to England for the rest of the winter. Those that remained worked in the sheds, preparing material and equipment for the resumption of work.

> By May of 1285 the curtain walls were rising once again, but still the only towers were those of the all-important gatehouse. Because these were the most vulnerable parts of the castle's defenses, Master James had planned them with great care and all the latest features.
>
> *Built to Last* by David Maccaulay (2010: Houghton Mifflin Harcourt), pg. 36

There's so much information here, but he keeps the focus on what's going on in the castle—he doesn't get into the economics or politics of having workers from England who had to return home each winter, for example. The questions—how far could they get and what happens in the winter—are what he answers.

As you can see even in this example, research questions most often lead you back to character and consequence. If the answer does not affect behavior, conflict, or decision-making, it may not belong on the page.

## Organizing your Research

Organizational tools help you keep things where you can find them again, in case it suddenly matters what kind of joinings your heroine's oak desk actually has.

The tools you use really depend on you. I have known writers to recommend Scrivener, Word documents, or a good old-fashioned filing cabinet chock full of photocopied pages. Some people create extensive story bibles in Google while others have spreadsheets to track world details. Once upon a time, I longed for a good database; now I use Word and depend heavily on the search function.

As you build your world, it also helps to keep the research you use in your story bible. We'll talk more about this later.

Research is not about accumulating trivia. It is about understanding systems deeply enough that you can choose what to include.

Research is fun. Most of us write because we love to share information, play with ideas, and learn new things. But first and foremost, we are writers. Your research should strengthen your world, not replace it.

In the next chapter, we will consider the opposite problem: how to know when to stop building and start writing.

## Reflection Questions

- What specific questions drove your current research?
- Are you gathering information because it affects your story, or because it is interesting?
- Which STAMP ON category feels least supported by research?
- In nonfiction, have you verified the systems that shape your narrative—economic, cultural, technological?
- Where might you be over-researching to avoid drafting?

## Exercise: Focused Research Plan

Choose one element in your project that requires clarification.

- Write three precise questions about it.
- Identify two sources you will consult (book, expert, article).
- Set a limit: one hour or one chapter of reading.
- Summarize what you learned in five sentences.

Note how that information changes—or does not change—your story. If you cannot articulate how the research affects your narrative, reconsider whether it is necessary.

CHAPTER SIX

# When to Stop Building and Start Writing

For some authors, worldbuilding and the research that goes with it is as much (or more) exciting than writing the actual book. There is always another layer to uncover, another article to read, another expert to consult. Curiosity feeds imagination, but that doesn't mean a thing to writing unless imagination feeds story.

A book is not built out of research. It is built out of the unique way you apply that research to the plot, characters, and settings that make your book the one readers remember with a smile.

You have already learned to ask STAMP ON questions. You have followed ripple effects. You have tested internal logic. Now comes what, for some, is the tougher skill: Knowing when to close the notebook and open the manuscript.

## Knowing When to Stop

Research can be a ton of fun, and there always seems to be one more question. In 2026, when I was researching Enceladus for a middle grade sci-fi, I had an hour-long conversation with a scientist who worked with the Casini probe about how the kids would move on the snowy moon. (It's tougher than you'd think!)

However, there comes a time, when you have to put the research aside and actually write the book. How do you know when that time has come?

When I was talking to the professor, I knew when my brain started flying in multiple "What if" directions (and the professor needing to go.) So, clue one is if you start confusing yourself, you may be in too deep. Step back, write a little, and see where the story takes you.

There is a difference between asking focused STAMP ON questions and spiraling into hypotheticals that do not serve the current scene. When your curiosity multiplies faster than your clarity, it may be time to return to the page.

On the other hand, you may come across a piece of research and—boom!—your brain ignites. You see the scene. You feel what the character is experiencing. You know what happens next. Don't waste the inspiration looking for one more paper-thin detail! Go to your story and write while the words demand to flow! The research will be there later. (Except if you are in the middle of a conversation, don't be rude—finish your talk, then write!)

*Inspiration is a signal.* When the research transforms into narrative energy, you have enough to move forward.

On the gripping hand (Pournelle and Niven, anyone?), you might find that your research is going nowhere. It may be interesting of itself, but if it's not feeding your story, then put the book aside, ask more questions, or start writing.

Save the book as a reward once you get your word count for the day done.

(BTW, the gripping hand is from *The Mote in God's Eye* by Larry Niven and Jerry Pournelle. The aliens in the story have three arms—two weaker left ones and a strong right one—the gripping hand. See how this one change went beyond physical and influenced even their logic and vernacular?)

## Research as an Avoidance Tactic

Sometimes, writing is intimidating. The story seems too big, or your real world is too distracted, and reading up feels like progress.

And it can be, but there's a difference between building knowledge and postponing writing. One sparks curiosity and inspires; the other breeds paralysis. If you are still researching the tensile strength of medieval rope but haven't drafted the scene in which the rope is used, you may want to ask yourself why.

While you're doing that, also ask what you can do about it. After all, asking "why" is research. "What can I do about it?" is action.

When the story itself is intimidating you, break it down. Do an outline of the next chapter or an overview of the entire book in simple form of character does x; character does y, etc. Sometimes, we dive into research because we don't know the path ahead.

If the story has stalled and research is not sparking any ideas for moving forward, ask your characters what's wrong. I do mean this literally. When I was stuck on *Live and Let Fly*, I went into my own imagination and asked the characters. It turned out one of the minor players didn't like her role. She was refusing to play it in my mind, and no amount of reading spy books or researching intelligence gathering methods was going to change the fact that she didn't want to be a spunky sidekick—she wanted to be a damsel in distress.

Once I gave in, the book wrote itself. It wasn't an issue of knowledge but of execution.

If the issue is time to write (because it's easier to read or take notes than to sit at the computer and immerse yourself into your own world), then you need to make changes to your routine or adjust your goals. Maybe negotiate for an hour in a coffee shop (not the library!) where you can write. Or maybe have a notebook handy as well as whatever textbook you have by your chair so you can write a sentence or two when the world is quiet and you can sit for 10 minutes.

If you sit at the computer and words won't come, try a different environment, talking your text, or handwriting.

Ditto if the problem is the distraction of the computer—you look away from your manuscript to Google something about whales, and the next thing you know an hour has passed, and somehow, you've read four articles and watched 11 YouTube videos, including three on corsets (because they used whalebone.) If that's your issue, I recommend simply putting a marker in your manuscript, and moving on. Here's an example from my current WIP:

> Jake yelped in surprise! "Holy cow! (describe how a head cut would look different in microgravity).

> "Easy!" Anna replied. "It probably looks worse than it is. Surface tension makes blood stick to things instead of flow (check fact). Zach, try not to move and when we get you free, don't sit up. Without gravity, your blood will flow to your head and make the bleeding worse."

Then after you've written all the words for the session, go back. (Hint: You can do this when you forget a secondary character's name or a characteristic like eye color so you don't lose momentum.)

The point is to not let research derail you from the actual writing itself.

Finally, beware getting encyclopedia syndrome. Knowing the full metallurgy of a sword is not the same as telling a compelling story in which that sword matters. Three pages on the blade's construction before the duel begins will not increase tension. It will dilute it.

## How Much Research Is Enough?

The amount of research required depends on the scale of your project.

- **Use case:** If you are writing an encyclopedia or a DnD manual or a bestiary (real or imagined), then you may need to do more research and more thinking. A textbook needs more research than a children's book on the same topic or a novel.
- **Audience:** If you are writing for an academic audience, they'll expect more detail, including background, implications and theory. The casual reader wants something more direct, if simpler.
- **Genre:** Hard science fiction needs to delve into the actual science and how things work. Space Opera is more in the realm of "potentially plausible but mostly cool." Compare, for example, *The Martian* by Andy Weir vs. *The Martian Chronicles* by Ray Bradbury vs. *John Carter of Mars* by Edgar Rice Borroughs.
- **Familiarity:** The more familiar the world you write in is, the less you need to deeply research. Like in the example in the previous section—you don't have to research how people bleed on Earth.

- **Size:** A short story often requires less research than a longer book or even a series. That's not always true, of course, but in short stories it's important to use each word wisely. There's less room for long explanations about why the curtains are blue.
- **Purpose of worldbuilding:** If the world is a backdrop for a tightly focused character study or a fast-moving adventure full of action, then you may need less background.

STAMP ON can help you gauge sufficiency. Have you addressed the categories that directly affect your plot? Have you ensured internal logic? Have you traced the primary ripple effects? If so, you may have enough to begin drafting.

In nonfiction, consider: Have you verified the systems that shape your narrative? Have you confirmed cultural practices, economic incentives, or technological constraints? Once those foundations are solid, get writing and delve into further research only as you need to refine or fill holes.

Worldbuilding is scaffolding. Research is the bricks. *Writing* is construction.

They all matter. But at some point, the walls must go up.

Next chapter, we'll talk about the art of writing and how to show readers your world without it becoming an encyclopedia entry.

## Reflection Questions

- Has your recent research clarified your story, or merely satisfied your curiosity?
- Which STAMP ON categories are fully developed for your current project?
- Which details have you researched but not used? How might you use them differently (marketing, new story, etc.)
- In nonfiction, are you including information because it is relevant, or because it was difficult to uncover?
- If you stopped researching today, could you draft the next scene with confidence?

## Exercise: The Research Line

Draw a line down a page.

- On the left, list the research you have completed.
- On the right, list the scenes you have written.

Now examine the balance.

If the left column is significantly longer, choose one researched element and draft a scene that uses it (even if it's not the next scene). If the right column is longer but you feel uncertain, identify the one question that blocks you and research only that question. Then return to drafting.

The goal is not to eliminate research. It is to keep it in proportion.

CHAPTER SEVEN

# Showing the World Through Your Characters

You've done it! You've researched all the systems of a world using STAMP ON, you've asked the questions, built the frameworks, and now you're ready to start writing. But how do you put all that beautiful research and worldbuilding into practice?

By letting the reader experience it naturally.

Readers do not walk into a world with a clipboard to check your work. They may be planning to take notes, especially in nonfiction, but if all they wanted was a summary and notes, they'd turn to AI summaries.

In fiction in particular, readers are there for a story—to live the life of your characters for a few entertaining hours. They don't want to pause the action to absorb an informational briefing. The want to experience a setting the same way they experience a person: gradually, through interaction.

The most natural way to reveal a world is through character point of view.

## Let Characters Tell You

How do you do this? It's simple: *Let your characters tell you what you need to know.*

This does not mean your character delivers a lecture (or if they do, it's because story demands it and even then, it's only the part of the lecture that builds tension, explains a moment more than a world, and foreshadows future events. And even then, it's done through their filter.

As the writer, you know the world and everything in it (for the most part), but that doesn't mean your character does or that your character cares. When you reveal the world to your reader, doing it in ways natural to the character not only makes the world accessible but draws the reader into the character.

A child in a restaurant will notice different things than the real estate agent there to sell it to a developer. A superspy will walk in and automatically note the exits and locations of potential threats. A working chef smells onions and notices how clean the oven is before noting the details on the light fixtures. The world appears filtered through lived priorities.

When detail arises from action and perception, it feels organic. When it appears independent of either, it feels inserted.

## Don't Make Your Characters Mouthpieces

Sometimes, especially when a writer has something they want to say, they will use their characters as mouthpieces for their own thoughts. This is especially tempting for people who are writing with a political or evangelical motivation. This could be because they are writing to a market (Christian fiction) or because their own convictions are driving them to the story.

Sometimes, the opposite is true. The writer wants to make a religious leader into a zealot or a hypocrite. Or they may take someone with a political or social ideology and mock them, make them especially stupid, or craft them as the villain because of their ideologies alone.

There's nothing wrong with fiction that has strong political or religious overtones. I myself am writing an expressly Catholic science fiction series that teaches the Heavenly Virtues. The danger comes when you let those convictions manipulate your characters like puppets in a show instead of letting them live out the adventures. This can come out in:

- **Sermonizing:** Whether in conversation or an outright speech, the character makes a passionate exposition for their belief.
- **Heavy-handed writing:** The villain is over-the-top evil in a way that you take time to explain and attribute to ideology: "He's a

pagan!" or "He's a Conservative!" Meanwhile, the good guys are so pure they wouldn't even dream of swearing or smoking or jaywalking or...

- **Miraculous Conflict Resolution:** The character faces trouble after trouble until that magic moment they accept your ideology and (cue angelic choir), their outlook is suddenly wonderful and everything gets solved like a 30-minute TV show.

While some readers (especially those who already agree with you) may be fine with this, it rarely goes down well with the average reader. That's because it's sloppy writing.

So what do you do? Avoid stereotypes. In part this is character crafting, which is beyond the scope of this book. On the other hand, using the world to show the character's motivation—instead of pinning it to "He's a Liberal!" gives that character depth. So will putting him in a situation where his good side shows—this can be especially powerful if the good side comes from the same motivation. An environmental terrorist, for example, might volunteer at the pound.

If your character would make a speech or have a deep conversation, be sparing. Keep it short, infuse reaction and interior thoughts, and make sure it's fully integral to the story—in a way that is causing real tension. Maybe the speech doesn't need to be shown in real-time, but in memories and call backs that draw the reader in until you share part of the speech—and then they eat it up.

If you have a point to make, by all means make it, but build it into your world so you don't have to preach. Use subtle cues, remember that characters always have some good and some bad and season them with that other element, and don't use ideology as the CureAll for whatever trouble the character faces.

Faith is a source of strength. Changing ideologies can signify growth. Both are valid parts of worldbuilding, but if you cram it down your reader's throat, you will lose them, not win them to your side.

## Specs or No Specs?

You most likely have knowledge your character doesn't, whether by research or imagination. Avoid the temptation to share the nifty details with the reader unless they're something the character would know.

For example, if your average civilian is thrust into a firefight where they have to defend themselves, they probably aren't going to know they just grabbed a Sig Sauer P320 which is normally a .40 caliber but that one was converted to 9mm for lower recoil. He's just going to know he grabbed a gun and shot the bad guy.

If a character (or narrator), in the middle of a firefight, pauses to describe the technical specifications of the weapon—the make, model, voltage output, production history—the moment collapses. The reader is no longer inside the scene but outside it, reading a catalog entry.

Can there be exceptions to this? Yes. In his *Monster Hunter International* books, Larry Correia takes great pleasure in his characters describing the weaponry they use against monsters, but the characters are also highly trained, and that knowledge is vital for their survival. Even so, Correia has said that when Baen took his book, the editors made him take out some of the more extraneous details.

In nonfiction, you need to consider your audience. An article about a new law, for example, will include more legal technicalities when written for a law magazine than for a public service announcement flyer.

## Details Have Consequences

Worldbuilding detail should enter the scene when it has consequence. Here's an example of cryogenics from *We are Legion: (We Are Bob)* by Dennis E. Taylor:

> "So… You'll cut my head off." I raised an eyebrow at the salescritter. I was baiting him. I knew it, he knew it, I knew he knew it.
>
> He grinned at me, happy to go along with the routine as long as me and my wallet continued to pay attention…

> The CryoEterna sales rep—the nametag identified him as Kevin—nodded and gestured toward the big placard, which displayed the cryonics process in ghoulish detail. I took a moment to note his Armani suit and hundred-dollar haircut. It appeared there was money in Cryonics.
>
> "Bob, there's no point in freezing the entire body. Remember, the idea is to wait for advancements in medicine to be able to cure whatever killed you. By the time they can resuscitate your corpse, they'll likely be able to grow you a whole new body. That would be easier, in fact, than trying to patch up the old one."
>
> *We are Legion: (We Are Bob)* by Dennis E. Taylor (2016: Worldbuilders Press), pg. 1

I don't know how much research Taylor did into cryogenics or what kind of "what if" questions he asked about the process, but I do know that he didn't tell us the gruesome details on the sales materials. The character didn't care. For that matter, the story didn't care. This is the story of Bob after revival.

...which means that the important things to know—the answers to Taylor's "what if"—are answered in the sales pitch: By the time humankind can revive him, technology will advance in ways we can only surmise.

Rather soon in the story, Bob is killed and wakes up over 100 years later as an AI.

We get more of the explanation, but only after Bob has had time to discover the clues: the strange perspectives in his vision, the mechanical sound of his voice, the doctor telling him to talk so it helps the GUPPI interface. Then as he starts to realize…

> "Right, so can we talk about how much of me is still human?...How much is Borg? Should I ask for a mirror, or would that be a bad idea?"
>
> "Ah…" Dr. Landers glanced down at his tablet… "…If I remember my Trek trivia correctly…Mr. Data would be a better comparison…. You, Bob, are what most people would call an Artificial Intelligence, although that's not strictly accurate. You are a copy of the mind of Robert Johansson, created by scanning his cryogenically frozen brain at the subcellular level and converting its data into a computer simulation. You are, essentially, a computer program that thinks it's Robert Johansson. A replicant."

"Does that mean I'm immortal, then?"

*We are Legion: (We Are Bob)* by Dennis E. Taylor (2016: Worldbuilders Press), pg. 19

Now there's more technical explanation because it's important to the story and the future plot. But more importantly, it's important to Bob. It's vital to his understanding his new life and everything that happens from now on. Note that despite all this, Bob homes in on what's important and interesting to him: *Am I immortal now?*

By concentrating on what's important to your character, you avoid getting yourself (and your reader) lost in the weeds of minutia and keep the story exciting.

## Emotional Reaction as Worldbuilding

Backstory often enters through emotion. You can show emotional reaction in many ways.

- **Characters can act it out:** If a character stiffens at the sight of a uniform, that tells us something about political authority and her experience with it in this world. If a woman gasps when entering a cathedral, you immediately feel the grandeur.

- **They can comment on it:** If a former factory worker curses the corporate name of his employer, we get a hint at past trouble that may have been broader than just him.
- **You can have interior comments:** In my book, *Neeta Lyffe, Zombie Exterminator,* Neeta wryly observes "There weren't enough swear words in the English language for her job." It gives you a feel not for the danger but the overall frustration and nastiness of fighting the undead as your day job.

The same thing applies to nonfiction. You often see this in celebrity interviews, where the reporter takes some time to comment on the person's relaxed state in their home, for example, and contrast it to the high-stress environment of the studio. Or consider how reporting about a burned apartment building will change if you do it from the point of view of the fire chief for a firefighters magazine as opposed to the local paper from the POV of someone who lost their home.

Worlds don't always have to be explained. Sometimes they are felt.

## Readers Discover Worlds the Way They Discover People

When you meet someone new, you don't exchange CVs or ask them to recite their family history. You have a conversation, do things together. Over time, you learn more and you notice more—gestures, tone, habits, priorities...

Worldbuilding works the same way.

If you frontload every historical and political detail, you deny the reader the pleasure of discovery. By the same token, if you withhold all context, you risk confusing them. The balance lies in layering.

*Storm Front* by Jim Butcher introduces the complex world of wizard Harry Dresden, who lives in Chicago but has connections to the world of magic. It doesn't start with an explanation of the world or the creatures or how magic works. It starts with him talking about his business, how people are more aware of the paranormal, but that business is slow. As the mystery happens, the world expands to include the Chicago police, how spells work, the creatures (good and evil)...but each shows up when the plot needs it. His world is crazy rich, but if he'd shared it all at once, the story would have been lost—and the world might not have been as immersive as a result.

In nonfiction, this layering is equally powerful. *Not a Good Day to Die: The Untold Story of Operation Anaconda* by Sean Naylor is an excellent example. Chapter 11 starts with Frank Wiercinski receiving an important phone call about an upcoming operation. Naylor takes time to describe the mundane details of the office before mentioning that the classified maps are in the operations room. The next paragraphs are about 9-11 and how it affected Wiercinski's career; then he brings in a brief overview of the 101st Airborne...all pieces of the puzzle that lead to the operation. He doesn't have to tell you this is important, you are pulled along the journey with Wiercinski.

Worldbuilding through POV respects the reader's intelligence. It allows inference.

## What About Third-Person Omniscient?

When you are the godlike narrator explaining the world to the eager reader, you have a special responsibility to make sure the things you share do multiple duty:

- Advance the plot
- Illuminate the characters or situation
- Add color or tone to the narrative

Here's an example from Douglas Adams, whose *Hitchhiker's Guide to the Galaxy* is a classic of sci-fi and humor. He's describing the moments before the Earth is destroyed.

> It's difficult to say exactly what the people on the surface of the planet were doing now, because they didn't really know what they were doing themselves. None of it made a lot of sense—running into houses, running out of houses, howling noiselessly at the noise. All around the world city streets exploded with people, cars skidded into each other as the noise fell upon them and then rolled off like a tidal wave over hills and valleys, deserts and oceans, seeming to flatten everything it hit.
>
> Only one man stood and watched the sky, stood with terrible sadness in his eyes and

rubber bungs in his ears. He knew exactly what was happening and had known ever since his Sub-Etha Sens-O-Matic had started winking in the dead of night beside his pillow and wakened him with a start. It was what he had waited for all these years, but when he had deciphered the signal pattern sitting alone in his small dark room, a coldness had gripped him and squeezed his heart. Of all the races in the Galaxy who could have come and said a big hello to planet Earth, he thought, didn't it just have to be the Vogons.

*Hitchhikers Guide to the Galaxy* by Douglas Adams (1979: Pocket Books), pgs. 33-34

- **Plot is advanced:** The Earth is in panic; the Vogons are an alien race
- **Character is illuminated:** One man knew and is sad about it, yet sardonic. He is probably an alien since he knows the Vogons and has a Sub-Etha Sens-O-Matic.
- **Tone is communicated:** We know this story will not be tragic so much as ironic and full of dry humor. We also know it's sci-fi, but rooted in our time.

As you share your world, even through your narrator view, remember that each detail you put in needs to serve the story somehow.

## What To Do With What You Don't Include

You worked hard for your research. You probably have more ideas than you can possibly share through your characters or plot. Alas, you have to resist the temptation to share everything. Too much exposition can halt momentum of the plot and make readers put the book down or skim. Both erode the immersive experience that readers want and appreciate.

Before including a detail, ask:

- Would this character notice this?
- Does this detail alter action or choice?
- Does it change the emotional landscape?

If the answer is no, it may belong in your notes rather than in the paragraph.

Fear not! There's a lot of potential in those extra notes:

- Use it for marketing material, like blogs, newsletters, or "About the World" posts on social media.
- Save the ideas for future books in that world.
- Adapt your notes to different stories.

Worldbuilding is not a catalog. It is a lived experience. When the world enters through character perception, it gains weight without demanding explanation.

In the next chapter, we will look at other tools—maps, language, documents—that can support this immersion without overwhelming it.

## Reflection Questions

- In your current manuscript, where does exposition interrupt action?
- Which details arise naturally from character perception?
- Are there technical explanations that could be replaced with demonstrated effects?
- In nonfiction, are you presenting context abstractly or through lived experience?
- What does your protagonist notice first in any new environment, and why?
- In nonfiction, are you keeping your reader's knowledge and experience in mind?

## Exercise: Rewrite for Consequence

Choose one paragraph of worldbuilding exposition from your draft.

Rewrite it twice:

- Through the lens of a character actively engaged in a scene.
- By replacing at least two descriptive facts with demonstrated effects. For example, instead of describing a weapon's specifications, show its recoil bruising the shoulder. Instead of explaining a factory's economic decline, show a worker staring at a silent assembly line.

Compare the versions. Which one feels inhabited?

CHAPTER EIGHT

# Other Ways to Show the World

Up to this point, we've focused on showing the world primarily through character point of view. While the strongest and most immersive method, it is not the only one. Nor does it have to work alone.

Writers have long used additional devices to deepen a setting: maps, invented language patterns, embedded documents, glossaries, and structural framing tools such as captain's logs or journal entries. These devices can enrich a story, clarify complex systems, and extend STAMP ON elements beyond the immediate scene.

Used thoughtfully, they expand the world without overwhelming the narrative. Used carelessly, they become distractions. The difference lies in purpose.

Let's examine those now.

## Maps

Maps are one of the most beloved worldbuilding tools in fantasy and science fiction. A beautifully drawn map elevates a book.

But a map should do more than look attractive. They provide orientation. They signal scope. They imply history, and done well, they visualize STAMP ON in spatial form.

Obviously, a map reflects Natural features (mountains, rivers, climate), but it can also show Political boundaries, Social and economic elements (churches, marketplaces). They can be used to show Military maneuvering and tactical weaknesses, and of course, they can hint at Animals (Here Be Dragons!).

Before creating a map, ask:

- Where do people live, and why there?

- What Natural rescources shape settlement?
- What barriers influence culture?
- Where would conflict logically arise?

If you do not intend to use the geography in the story, a detailed map may be unnecessary. If rivers, borders, or distances drive plot, then mapping becomes functional rather than merely decorative.

Creating a map does not require artistic mastery. Many writers begin with rough sketches—boxes for towns, lines for rivers. Digital tools exist to create maps, but a pencil and notebook work just as well. I've even seen memes where people photograph things like spills and potholes and use the outlines to form their land.

Nowadays, it's possible to feed these drawings into AI or other map-generating tools and create a lovely image from your chicken scratchings.

Regardless, the purpose is clarity for the writer first, beauty for the reader second.

*The Lord of the Rings* includes detailed maps that reinforce travel distance, terrain hardship, and political fragmentation. The map is not ornamental. It structures the journey.

Nonfiction uses mapping differently but just as effectively. History books, naturally, include maps to orient readers within campaigns or growing empires. Sometimes maps are used to clarify a concept, like we often see in elections where the map is colored by which party took which state. A visual representation can take a long explanation and compress it into something people get immediately.

Map can answer questions the story actually raises.

Maps can set a tone, too. A land marked "Forbidden Forest" makes you think mystery and adventure. A land marked "Bad idea-nope!" most likely signals irony and humor.

And that leads us to language.

## Language Quirks and Naming

Language, as in terms and slang, can tell you a lot about a society—what it considers important, worthwhile, or heinous. It can signal forbidden topics and moral taboos.

Let's look at a real-world example: Chinese. Did you know that the number 250 is a curse word in Chinese? If you call someone 250, you are saying they are stupid and useless. "Selling tofu" is a euphemism for prostitution.

When I was writing *Zach Augustine*, a middle grade book for Pauline Books and Media, a Catholic publisher, the nuns asked me to come up with a different way to say "stupid." The book takes place near Saturn around 100 years in the future. My husband came up with lowram—low RAM, implying diminished processing power. (Is it bad that I hope some geeky kid will call his nemesis "lowram"?) I also decided "dustbrained" worked, since Zach came from the asteroid belt, and dust is not a great thing to have.

In addition to new worlds, accent, syntax, and idioms can tell you a lot. For example, the elves in my *DragonEye, PI* series are long-lived; as a result, they are more willing to spend time on pleasantries and have a whole regimen for speaking that includes deeply acknowledging the person they're talking to—from family history to current situation. Incidentally, this not only became a defining characteristic and a long-running comic trope, but also resulted in a new threat—diet sodas that alter their brain chemistry and make them talk with human brevity.

When it comes to terminology, there's a simple rule: *Don't create a colorful language at the expense of readability.* If it's got an Earth equivalent, use the Earth name. Call a shoe a shoe. If it's unique to your world, give it a new name.

Invented vocabulary should serve clarity, not obscure it. If readers must decode every noun, they get thrown out of the story instead of drawn in. If terminology emerges only when necessary, it enriches rather than burdens.

At the same time, restraint matters. A page of untranslated terms slows momentum. A few well-chosen linguistic markers establish tone.

There are exceptions, of course. Consider the opening lines of *A Clockwork Orange* by Anthony Burgess:

> There was me, that is Alex, and my three droogs, that is Pete, Georgie, and Dim, Dim being really dim, and we sat in the Korova Milkbar making up our rassoodocks what to do with the evening, a flip dark chill bastard though dry.
>
> *A Clockwork Orange* by Anthony Burgess (1995: W. W. Norton & Company), pg. 1

He uses his invented slang, Nadsat, to immerse readers in the subculture. It can feel very confusing at first, but he works hard to create context to give you the gist, if not the meaning, of the words—"three droogs, that is Pete, Georgie, and Dim" lets you know "droogs" are friends rather than animals, while "the evening, a flip dark chill bastard though dry" lets you now the weather is cold but not humid. The language builds world through immersion rather than explanation.

It doesn't always have to be made up, either, but researched. Burgess pulled from Russian—in fact *nadsat* means "-teen" in Russian.

I wonder what he might thing of "brain rot," the slang of GenAlpha.

If you are writing historical fiction and want real authenticity, you might go back and look for more original words—and check what words and phrases were not around. (This is fun, too. Did you know in Victorian times, to say something was perfect, you'd say it's "bang up the elephant"?)

You might also want to clear out modern slang. Even something as simple as "that's not my problem," might be too blunt for your era.

If you are into research and love to read, go find books written in the time or find diaries or correspondence from that era.

In nonfiction, language can tell a reader what region you're writing about. This is especially true when quoting people, especially if you want to highlight a dialect (but don't go overboard, or you risk insulting the speaker—sometimes, it's better to say "thick Southern accent").

It's not really worldbuilding, but as long as we're discussing language in nonfiction, I'd like to note that it also sets the tone. If you are going for something academic, you will use larger and more technical or precise words than if you are writing a fun commentary.

That doesn't mean you can't be academic and funny. Here're two history books. One is written for a college classes, and the other for the casual reader. Both are funny (IMHO) and both use source documents:

> In enumerating the prodigies which, in the winter of 218-219 B.C., preluded the invasion of Hannibal, Livy mentions without further comment the incident of an ox which escaped from the cattle market and scaled the stairs of a riverside insula to fling itself into the void from the third story to the horrified cries of the onlookers.
>
> *Daily Life in Ancient Rome* by Jerome Carcopino (1940: Yale University Press), pgs. 24-25

Now compare the tone to…

> The number of Hannibal's elephants, thirty-seven, is said by Polybius to have been inscribed by Hannibal's own hand on a brazen plate in Italy. Polybius read it himself. Yet a modern historian has recently given the figure as forty, perhaps from a natural tendency to deal in round

numbers. Elephants do not come in round numbers.

*The Decline and Fall of Practically Everybody* by Will Cuppy (1992: Barnes & Nobles Books, although the copyright is 1950, just 10 years after *Daily Life in Ancient Rome*), pg. 51

Language is one of the most efficient worldbuilding tools available.

One more note about language: In this litigious society, you (or your publisher) may be afraid of being sued if you use common brands in your stories. Disney and Paramount are especially vigilant about protecting their trademark. I won't get into common use law here. Rather, I'll just say that this is another time when you may want to make up your own words for items, like light sabers or tricorders or store names.

## Historical Documents and Embedded Texts

Another way to deepen a world is to embed documents within the narrative: decrees, letters, newspaper clippings, religious texts, court transcripts. Sometimes, you see these as "excerpts" quoted with the chapter heading. Other times, they'll only be referred to by the characters without actually quoting them.

Whichever way you handle them, these documents suggest history, reveal laws and procedures, or provide social commentary.

These can also be a lot of fun to write, but when using them, be sure they serve the story. If you write a peace treaty between your two countries, then it only needs to be brought up when there's an issue that threatens that peace. I have a list of rules and philosophies for my spacers, the Spacer's Code, but it's only ever mentioned piecemeal, when someone needs to be reminded of a certain rule.

Sometimes, these documents can create the structure of the story, such as *Dracula* by Bram Stoker. It's an epistolary novel, which means the story is told through letters, journal entries, and news clippings. Stoker used this familiar, realistic format of everyday communication to highlight the supernatural, which makes the horror feel somehow more real.

Nonfiction, of course, regularly employs embedded documents. Court transcripts, diary excerpts, and archival letters bring immediacy to historical analysis. (We saw this above in *Daily Life in Ancient Rome*.) They can give readers a glimpse into the actual world of the writer of the time.

Even so, you should only include what advances the reader's understanding. That can be hard to do, especially if you spent hours finding that one document and it's so cool. Like with all research, don't discard it; use it for something else!

## Captain's Logs and Framing Devices

Captain's logs, journal entries, field notes, and mission briefings offer another controlled lens for presenting information.

These devices justify exposition because they exist within the story's logic. Ship captains dictate status updates. Scientist record observations. Journalists write articles.

However, these tools should not become convenient dumping grounds for information.

Generally, a framing tool provides some quick background or foreshadowing. However, they are at their best when they do multiple duties—worldbuilding, tone setting, and set-up. Here's an example

> Captain's Personal Log, Intergalactic Date 676786.68
>
> We're back on patrol again after a brief stop at the Union's station at Argo for some repairs, and to rub it in the face of the Union fleet that we defeated a Cyber hive while they were on a wild goose chase. It was all the funnier that some of the captains didn't have a cultural reference for geese, wild or otherwise.
>
> *Space Traipse: Hold My Beer* by Karina Fabian (2019: Laser Cow Press), pg. 77

From this, you know:

- The Impulsive just succeeded in a dangerous mission, most likely alone
- There's a known enemy called the Cybers that has a hive-mind (though you might think they're insects from just this piece)
- They are part of a larger fleet with stations and aliens who don't have waterfowl
- The Captain is proud and has a sense of humor
- Their mission is patrol, implying the Union is not a totally peaceful place and the fleet is at least semi-military in mission
- There's going to be some humor

This log takes place after the first story, but notice how I didn't recap the fight with the Cybers. To do so makes it redundant and not worth the reader's time.

If the captain's log recaps events the reader has just witnessed, it becomes redundant. However, it can provide insight into how the captain sees the events, building tension or foreshadowing future.

> Captain's Log, Intergalactic Date, 676768.69

> Prince Petru has apparently fallen in love with our xenologist and ship's sexy, Loreli. Not that anyone can blame him, but it's making it hard to complete our mission of marrying him off to the princess of his neighboring world and thus ensuring peace in the system. Not to mention the fact that he's become a nuisance. He will not take her "no" for an answer, and LaFuente's "stay the hell away from her" only seems to egg him on. For now, we've assigned Loreli a 24-hour security detail and are looking for alternatives to discourage the impetuous prince.
>
> *Space Traipse: Hold My Beer* by Karina Fabian (2019: Laser Cow Press), pg. 27

In nonfiction, similar framing appears in structured reports or reflective essays. A writer might open with a field journal entry from the explorer of the area they're writing about, or use a famous quote that sets the tone. For example, in *Hellhound On His Trail: The Electrifying Account of the Largest Manhunt In American History*, Hampton Sides begins Chapter One with a quote from Martin Luther King, Jr. to foreshadow the topic of the plight of the black man in 1967 Memphis.

## Glossaries and Appendices

Glossaries and appendices are especially useful in expansive or linguistically complex worlds. If your world is so fast that you're afraid your reader might not keep up with it, an appendix can provide them a quick way to make sure they remember who ruled which country or what exactly a *bladstak* is.

They can also be fun. When I did a glossary for my first *DragonEye, PI* book (by request of the publisher), I made all the descriptions in Vern's snarky voice. So instead of just blandly saying that elves live to be hundreds of years and thus have a leisurely way of conversing, Vern tells you they're long-lived and thus long-winded and take half an hour to ask where the bathroom is.

If you use a glossary or appendix, do not depend on the reader using it to understand the story. It should never replace narrative clarity. After all, the reader is there to be immersed in your world, not study it like a math book.

Appendices can also be a clever way to provide additional information not needed for the plot. In *The OSIRIS War*, Matthew P. Schmidt uses an appendix to give short summaries of what happened to all the main characters after the war. You see this in nonfiction, too, especially biographical movies.

In nonfiction, glossaries and appendices can be used for additional edification or even further education. They are equally helpful when discussing specialized industries or technical subjects. They allow writers to maintain narrative flow while offering reference support for readers who might need a little more explanation than their target reader.

## Visual Storytelling: Cartoonists and Graphic Novelists

Visual storytelling through comics or manga still requires worldbuilding, and many of the principles are the same, even when they don't result in the written word. You may still have to do research, ask "What if" and consider all the aspects in STAMP ON.

However, all of that is revealed in illustration and tight dialogue. A space-age skyline communicates technology level. A boarded-up storefront with an aging FOR SALE sign tells the reader that the economy is bad. A uniform communicates hierarchy—and depending on the style, can even suggest era and whether the regime is good or evil.

Panel composition also gives clues. In *Tales of Honor* by Top Cow Productions, Inc., you can tell by the size and clean, almost utilitarian spaceships that this is a disciplined military. The Medusa Surface NPA Headquarters, on the other hand, are natural, even archaic—wood slats, moss on the roof and walls. Not knowing the story, you'd surmise this is temporary or that the planet itself is not advanced.

The use of colors tells a lot, too. Tone-wise, they convey calm, seriousness, or urgency. The ship's colors tend toward blue, grey, and beige—very artificial, while the planet is far more natural as it should be. It also tells of a more technological world, whereas the *Firefly* comics by Titan Books are more comfortable and lean toward browns and greens, invoking a more "earthy" and Western feel.

Extra documents and framing techniques are also useful shorthands where every word counts. For example, *Watchmen* by Alan Moore and Dave Gibbons uses background newspapers, posters, and even graffiti to construct an alternate political climate without halting the plot.

In graphic novels, there are whole new ways to show your world. Nonetheless, since brevity and clarity are even more important, you need to be sure details reinforce character and conflict.

Whether through prose or illustration, worldbuilding succeeds when it integrates seamlessly with narrative movement.

Supplemental tools can expand your world gracefully. In some cases, like *Dracula*, they may even tell the story. However, you need to use them with deliberation so that they don't distract the reader instead.

Next chapter, we'll talk about worldbuilding for a standalone book or a series and how to track the details.

## Reflection Questions

- Would a map clarify geography that currently feels vague? How much do you need it? Does the reader need it?
- Are you inventing more terminology than your story requires?
- Could an embedded document reveal history more efficiently than dialogue?
- In nonfiction, could a visual aid or excerpted primary source strengthen immersion?
- Are supplemental materials enhancing the narrative, or compensating for weak integration within scenes?

## Exercise: Choose One Supplement

Select one device—map, glossary entry, embedded document, or language quirk. Create a brief sample:

- Sketch a simple map showing only locations relevant to your plot.
- Write a one-paragraph fictional decree that reveals a political tension.
- Draft a captain's log entry or other appropriate report that introduces a complication.
- Create three glossary entries.

Afterward, ask: Does this deepen the reader's understanding of STAMP ON systems, or merely decorate them—or worse, distract from the story?

If it deepens understanding, keep refining.

CHAPTER NINE

# Story Bibles, Continuity, and the Dreaded Retcon

We've gone really deep into worldbuilding, so I want to pause here and reiterate: Not every world needs to be built to the same depth.

If you're writing a short story about a child in her backyard, you may not need all the scaffolding STAMP ON suggests. If your adventure is straightforward, then perhaps a few "What if" questions will suffice.

You need more as your worlds get farther from the norm, your adventures get more complex, and your story gets longer. Series, in particular, benefit by some deep worldbuilding beforehand.

Trust me. I learned this the hard way. The moment you write Book Two, your world stops being a backdrop and becomes a record, and records require management.

Let's take some time to talk about scale, keeping records, and what to do when you need to start fresh.

## Scaling Depth: How Much World Does This Story Need?

Personally, I do enough worldbuilding to get the story moving. Then I let the characters tell me what I need to know about the world.

For the most part, that approach works beautifully for a short story or even a standalone book. You build what the plot demands. You answer STAMP ON questions only as they arise. The world grows in proportion to the story. You may have to go back and revise as something important pops up, but that's what second drafts and editing are for.

The moment readers return to that world, however, expectations shift. If it's in Book One, it can't be contradicted or replaced in Book Two with something completely different (unless there's a reason in-world that makes sense.) Your one-book isolated setting is now a series ecosystem.

When I wrote the short story, *"DragonEye, PI,"* it was supposed to be a one-off. Just a cute idea, but I got asked to do more stories about my main character, Vern, and then he grew in my mind and started telling me more about himself and his world. Which, of course, meant he needed the world to interact in and to define him.

What started out as a relatively shallow world with a portal, a stereotypical evil lair, a princess in distress, and a grumpy dragon PI on the wrong side of the portal, turned into something rich and layered:

- Because I mentioned his fight with St. George, I needed a Faerie Catholic Church
- Because there was a portal between the worlds and I needed a reason for Vern to

stay here even when he didn't like it, I needed Faerie politics

- Because he's a magical creature, I needed at least some general idea of how and why magic worked in our world
- Because I didn't want to deal with a world of new wizards, etc., (and because I'm Catholic) I needed a reason why humans can't practice magic (without turning to Satan)
- I had elves from my first story, but Vern started talking about all kinds of other creatures, and of course, I needed new foes for him each book

All this because a grumpy dragon wouldn't leave me alone—and people liked him! For a while, I went piecemeal, using my usual "write and find out" style of worldbuilding. That didn't work after a while, but we'll discuss that under retconning. Suffice to say, my poor worldbuilding stalled my writing for years because I was dealing with stuff I only sort-of knew.

Series writing exposes soft spots in worldbuilding. What you once hand-waved now matters.

When you're writing, keep a feel for the story and characters. Might you write more about them later? You may want to think about scaling.

Scaling depth means asking:

- Is this world a stage set, or is it an ongoing civilization?
- If I write more stories, where might they go? (This could mean socially vs. geographically, or it could mean growth in one area.)

If it is ongoing, STAMP ON systems must be tracked over time. For that matter, so should characters, events, and other important details.

That's where a story bible comes in.

## What about Nonfiction?

Nonfiction, especially across multiple articles or books, needs careful detail management even more than fiction. If Book One establishes economic causes for a conflict, Book Two cannot ignore them. If Part One documents regulatory failure, Part Two must account for subsequent reform.

Continuity in nonfiction is credibility.

*The Gulag Archipelago* by Aleksandr Solzhenitsyn is a three-volume "literary-investigation" detailing the Soviet forced labor camp system. He based it not just on his own experience but on over 227 testimonies. Nonetheless, he maintained narrative and political continuity across volumes by carefully tracking policy shifts, institutional structures, and personal testimonies over time. It's considered a literary and historical masterpiece.

Series nonfiction demands as much structural care as epic fantasy.

## Continuity Management: The Story Bible

Maybe you can keep track of details from book one to book two. I've written trilogies where I've not had to take copious notes even when the world is complex. Sometimes, I'd have to go back and read a section of a book, but that's always fun, anyway.

However, when *DragonEye, PI* grew to two books and a half-dozen stories, I began to lose track of characters and events, slang, and even the names of everyday items I changed the names for (like Xinga instead of Facetime).

I really needed to take better notes. And that meant a story bible.

## Creating a Story Bible

A story bible is not an encyclopedia or something you would share with your readers. Rather it's a living document that tracks everything from character names to timelines of events to story summaries. The key is they should make it easy to find any information you need from a past book.

Your story bibles can differ from series to series. For example, my *DragonEye* story bible contains:

- Human Characters
- Magicals (those that need magic to live)

- Dragons
- Elves
- Brand names
- Organizations
- Mundane social media
- Items from Faerie
- Places in Faerie
- Los Lagos & Mundane places
- Faerie slang
- Vern's Sayings
- Major events
- Faerie rituals
- Vern's growth by book
- Grace's growth by book

For *Space Traipse*, I have

- Intergalactic Dates (the format and the ones listed in Captain's Logs)
- People
- Places
- Ships
- Glossary (alien species, objects, etc.)
- Slang
- Imposazine doses
- Dour's favorite sayings
- Songs used against the Cybers

It all depends on what you need or find important for your particular series. If you don't know where to start, I suggest using STAMP ON to uncover the important aspects, then add characters, language, and a timeline if needed.

In addition, I have a separate story bible that covers each story with a summary, timeline, characters, and worldbuilding items. I use AI for this one, putting in a chapter and giving it a prompt. Be careful to read the responses. AI does not get intent and at times had fully hallucinated a chapter with baffling results.

However, it is a nice shortcut if you are building a story bible from scratch after already having written multiple books.

## What do entries look like?

What information should you include? Whatever you think you might likely forget or feel unsure about. If that's the color of your main character's eyes, then note it. If it's the name of the boyfriend's ship, record it.

I also suggest keeping track of what book or story the detail was mentioned in. That way, if you need to go back for more information, you know where to go.

You don't have to make it neat, BTW. My story bible is a mess of phrases, asides, jokes—even direct quotes from the book. Here's an example from my *Space Traipse* story bible:

> 101 Ways to Save a First Contact Gone FUBAR – Loreli's lecture at a xenologist convention (Foot in the Door)
>
> Actuaries - the Actuaries, lived for statistical research and reducing risks. Unfortunately, they'd done such a good job reducing risks that they'd run out of things to study except why their species was too bored to breed. So everyone lived long, secure, and incredibly unmotivated lives. Then came the Union, and specifically, the human race, who are anything but dull and secure. The Actuaries found new meaning to their lives. After only a few years, they also realized it would take generations to figure out humans. Their population experienced its first baby boom and has been thriving since. (Lone Star)

Altonian Schrodinger code - to compensate for the stacked overflow of stringly typed Heisenberg algorithm when cybercoding

I use Headers in Word to organize the sections, and then put entries in alphabetical order. Even so, sometimes I need to use the search function to find something. They are that big now. I have 200 characters in my *Space Traipse* series. (This is why I can't remember the names of real people I meet!)

## Using a Story Bible

At the time I'm writing this, I'm on Book 10 of my *Space Traipse* series. When I need an alien for background or a crewman to step up, I often open up my story bible. But a story bible is about more than details. It's about continuity.

This is important, because readers, especially those who come later to a series and binge your books, will notice the discontinuities.

*Star Trek* is a great example. Each new series gets run over the coals for any mistakes it makes to canon, whether it's totally ignoring a key aspect of a species or tossing in a side character species that should no longer exist.

When a series maintains continuity, however, the results can be spectacular. *The Expanse* series by James S.A. Corey (the pen name of authors Daniel Abraham and Ty Franck) is a textbook example. The world is rich and complex, with everything from Belter dialect to political intrigue that spans the solar system and all the books. But in each book, the decisions of the previous one have a direct effect on the next book. The growth feels organic, realistic—and that makes it engrossing. Incidentally, Daniel Abraham and Ty Franck were the writers and producers of *The Expanse* TV series to ensure the show stayed true to the books.

## The Importance of Timeline Tracking

As your series grows, so do the events in your book. Even if you don't have specific dates attached to your stories, it's a good idea to keep track of them.

There are lots of ways to do this:

- Real dates
- Made-up calendar dates
- Based off someone's age
- Starting from your inciting incident
- By book and chapter

The important thing is to track the event for cause and effect.

Without timeline notes, it's easy to forget an event and later negate it or decide to have it happen again. This can be an issue when you forget a battle or legal action, but it can also be a problem for minor details—your seven-year-old in Book Two is six in Book Three. It can also keep you from using the same trope, like your main character breaking the same arm four books in a row.

In nonfiction, timeline tracking is even more critical. If you are writing a historical account or investigative series, dates and cause-and-effect relationships must align. Readers will check, and if you make a mistake, you lose credibility.

## Retconning: When the Past Needs Adjustment

Sometimes, you just have to start over.

This is what happened with my *DragonEye, PI* series. I had a bunch of stories and two books—a truly jumbled mess as I chased whatever caper interested me or anthology wanted a Vern story. When I decided to get serious about the series, though, I was left with contradictions, a messed up timeline, and characters that didn't fit their own past.

Fortunately, the series wasn't especially popular and I was able to start from scratch, revise all my stories, and republish them. I gave myself complete freedom, so that one story grew into a full novel, while the first and second novels from the original timeline were revised as books 10 and 11.

However, if you don't have that luxury, there's always retconning. Retroactive continuity adjustment—retconning—means introducing something new in your story to explain a discrepancy from the past.

Retconning may be needed because a rule was badly defined or not well established, a necessary event contradicts the past, or a throwaway detail becomes structurally important.

The key is transparency within the narrative. Adjustments should feel like deeper understanding, not denial of prior events.

*Dr. Who* is a prime example. At first the Gallifreyans were just a highly advanced but human people, then it was revealed they had two hearts—but the first Doctor only had one heart. So they retconned in that they get the second heart after their first regeneration. They are also only supposed to have a limited number of regenerations, but time and again, The Doctor has found a way around that with some hitherto unknown methodology that was always there, but just never came up. The result: We can continue to watch our beloved Doctor as he has adventures in time and space.

Now, how does this differ from the lambasting *Star Trek* gets? Too often, they simply don't acknowledge the change or give a reason that also contradicts canon. Even for those of us who faithfully watch, anyway, it annoys!

One is sloppy writing. The other is responsible maintenance.

I hope you never have to revise or retcon your series, but if you do, take heart. The process can be fun and liberating. Revising Vern has made room for his growth as a character as well as bringing him a whole bunch of friends to interact with. He even has a DnD group now. Overall, he's a happier dragon, even if he does complain.

Wow—we've covered a lot. Let's take a quick look at how it all fits together.

## Reflection Questions

- Is your current project intended as a standalone or a series?
- Which STAMP ON categories would need expansion if you wrote a sequel?
- Do you have a centralized document tracking the important details of your book?
- Have you contradicted yourself across drafts? If so, can you revise or retcon?
- In nonfiction, are your cause-and-effect relationships chronologically clear?

## Exercise: Build a Mini Story Bible

Create a one-page continuity sheet for your current project.

Include:

- A timeline of major events
- A list of political or religious structures
- A short note on technological or magical limits
- Character ages and relationships

If writing nonfiction, include:

- Timeline of key events
- Policy or institutional changes
- Cause-and-effect chain

Then ask yourself: *If I wrote a sequel tomorrow, what would break first?* That answer tells you where your scaffolding is weakest.

CHAPTER TEN

# Bringing It All Together

By this point, you have built a world from multiple angles.

- You have put your STAMP ON it.
- You have asked "What if?" and traced consequences.
- You have checked internal logic.
- You have researched what matters to get you started, trusting that the story will show you the holes.
- You are showing the world through character rather than lecturing about it.

- You're making sound decisions on what to include and how to include it, and leaving the rest of your research and ideas for later use.
- You have decided whether the world must sustain one story or many.

What remains is balance.

Worldbuilding is not a separate task from storytelling. It is the architecture that supports it. Too little structure and the story is thin or the series collapses in chaos. Too much visible scaffolding and the reader never enters the building.

The art lies in proportion. So before you close the book and start on your own, let's review.

## STAMP ON Is Structure, Not Spotlight

STAMP ON gives you seven lenses: Social, Technological, Animals (and plants, insects, etc.), Military, Political, Origin story, Natural environment.

It's a way of asking, "What systems exist here?"

The answer to that is in the story itself, so let the story determine how much you worldbuild.

If the story is about a sea monster attacking a Scottish village, imperial politics may remain a backdrop, if it's mentioned at all, but if the story is about diplomatic collapse between Iraq and the United States, then political and religious structures must be more fully developed.

Structure serves story. It doesn't compete with it. Letting the story determine how much you worldbuild prevents half the common problems in fiction and nonfiction alike.

## Ripple + Logic + POV

Early in the book, we asked "What if?" Later, we insisted on internal logic. Then we narrowed our lens to character POV.

Those are not separate stages. They are filters.

Ripple thinking prevents simplistic alterations that make no impact, like Jovians who are merely shorter humans despite crushing gravity.

Internal logic dictates that a heavy-planet human will have a different bone density, a stronger heart to force blood up to the brain, and when they are in lower gravity, they will experience effects possibly similar to the astronauts in microgravity, but to a lesser degree.

The Iraqi guard example illustrates the same principle. Knowing that devout Muslims pray toward Mecca is not enough; understanding how that practice operates in real life matters.

POV ensures we feel the differences through their disorientation or need to move more carefully rather than learning about them through a physics lecture. When in omniscient mode, then the pressure is to impart adopt a POV that uniquely uses the right details at the right time to serve story and audience.

Research without nuance produces stereotype. Nuance without narrative produces exposition. Narrative without structure produces contradiction.

The systems must work together.

## Backstory Must Remain Backstory

Backstory needs to be BACKstory—let it inform the book, not become the book.

This is where many writers lose balance.

Just like with characters, worlds can have fascinating backstories that we'd love to share, but have no place in the book. The key to balance is weaving the important parts into the story when and where they illuminate a point or push the action forward. Keep the rest and use it for supporting matter—newsletters, social media, lead magnet stories.

That discipline applies equally in nonfiction. A historian may delve into decades of detailed political maneuvering. An investigative reporter may accumulate binders of statistics. Not all of it belongs in the chapter or article.

Restraint is not a lack of depth. It is clarity.

## Avoiding Extremes

Worldbuilding exists on a scale.

At one end, the world is peripheral.

At the other, the world is the story itself. In *The City and the Dungeon* by Matthew P. Schmidt, the world is so much more than a backdrop—everything about it from the layout to the complex rules the characters follow to navigate it—drive the story.

In my *Madness of Kanaan* series, the world of Kanaan literally is a character—making demands on its leader like a superpowered toddler as it fights for its own survival.

Most stories fall between those poles. Your task is not to force an extreme but to determine where your story lives and treat the world accordingly. A short mystery set in contemporary Illinois does not require invented cosmology. A multi-volume epic with cross-cultural theology does.

Proportion is the skill that makes your world enhance a story rather than distract from it.

## Nonfiction: The Same Architecture

We already know that even nonfiction histories have an element of worldbuilding when done well.

*Not a Good Day to Die* does this skillfully, weaving in mundane details, history, and real lives into a compelling history of Operation Anaconda.

That is STAMP ON at work in nonfiction: Social pressure, Political power, Technology, and Origin Story converging.

The same discipline applies: Research supports story; it does not replace it.

## A Master Checklist

When you feel uncertain about your balance, ask:

- Have I considered all relevant STAMP ON systems?
- Have I traced the ripple effects of my major alterations?

- Does my world obey its own internal logic?
- Am I showing the world through character POV? Or if omniscient/narrative POV, am I adopting a tone best suited for story and audience and using worldbuilding to support that?
- Is backstory informing the scene rather than interrupting it?
- Am I building only as much depth as this story requires?
- If writing a series, am I tracking continuity?

If you can answer those questions honestly and positively, you are likely in proportion.

Worldbuilding is not about quantity. It is about coherence.

When structure, ripple, logic, and perspective align, the world no longer calls attention to itself. It simply feels real.

And that isn't just good enough—that's the sweet spot that makes your world continue living beyond the pages of the book.

## Reflection Questions

- How satisfied are you with your worldbuilding?
- Have you confused structural depth with visible exposition?
- In nonfiction, are you presenting systems through lived experience or through summary?
- If you removed half your worldbuilding details, would the story still function? If so, which half?

## Exercise: The Integration Pass

Choose one scene from your current draft. Review it through four passes:

**Pass One: STAMP ON**

What systems are present but invisible?

**Pass Two: Ripple**

What consequences of earlier changes should be felt here?

**Pass Three: Logic**

Does anything contradict established rules?

**Pass Four: POV**

Is every detail something the character would notice? Or for omniscient, does it serve the reader in tone and need?

Revise only what fails one of these tests. Do not add more worldbuilding. Refine what is already there.

CHAPTER ELEVEN

# Your World Will Keep Living

By now, you know how to build a world. In fact, you may have taken apart a world and put it back together several times.

You've looked at it through STAMP ON and seen how those systems interact.

You've asked, "What if?" and watched consequences ripple outward. You've tested for internal logic, removed overexplaining, and are letting your characters reveal what matters. You've researched just enough and then had the good sense to close the book and start writing.

And if you're lucky, at some point, you stopped thinking about the framework and started to live in the world you've built.

If not, don't worry—once you get writing or polishing your story, you will. A finished world does not feel like a checklist. It feels inhabited.

When Vern began, he wasn't designed to carry an entire theological and political ecosystem. He was there to solve a mystery, save a princess, and snark a lot. But dragon shoulders are big—even when St. George shrunk him to pony size. His world expanded because it had to—because he demanded room to live.

The expansion wasn't planned in detail from the beginning. It came because stories (or more to the point, one beloved character) dictated it.

That is how most living worlds develop. Not from encyclopedic ambition, but from love.

You've probably experienced that yourself. You write a throwaway line and suddenly, you know the sequel to the story. A character makes a decision that demands future consequence that goes beyond his own life. A religious custom that once colored the background becomes integral to the character and thus needs developing

That growth is healthy, as long as the structure underneath can support it. As long as you think about the consequences. As long as you make sure you keep continuity from one book to the next so that the reader can stay immersed and live in your world as if it were real. You know how to do that, now. You have the tools.

You've also learned the opposite lesson: You don't need to explain everything. Backstory needs to stay BACKstory—let it inform the book, not become the book.

Do that and you honor your reader. You show that you trust them with your world and invite them to discover it the way they make a new friend—gradually, through interaction.

Nonfiction writers can build worlds just as surely as fantasy novelists do. Worldbuilding can bring context to data, empathy to cold facts, or a familiar framework on which to pin complex information. It allows readers to understand why events unfolded as they did and why they could not have unfolded otherwise.

That "could not have" is the mark of a well-built world. It suggests inevitability born of structure.

You do not have to create a universe balanced on elephants to be a worldbuilder. Worlds are built in sandboxes and cloudy skies, and the richer and truer you make your world within itself, the more your reader will want to remain in that world with you.

Trust is the quiet reward of careful worldbuilding.

It is also what allows you to step away, because you aren't leaving it to die, but to thrive in the mind of another—though if you're lucky, it will grow in your mind, too, driving you to the next story.

In the meantime, readers will move through your world as if it had always existed. When they close the book, they'll still carry the place with them, perhaps wondering what lies beyond the mountains or how the next election will unfold.

That wondering is not a failure to explain. It is a sign that the world is alive.

And when it feels alive, you have done enough.

# The Write Boost

## Practical Writing and Marketing Guides for Growing Writers

The Write Boost: Practical Writing and Marketing Guides for Growing Writers is a series of short, focused eBooks designed to help beginning and early-intermediate writers strengthen their writing craft and build real momentum. Each volume tackles one essential skill—from worldbuilding to editing, goal-setting to critique groups, idea generation to author marketing—with clear instruction, real examples, and practical exercises you can use right away.

Written by award-winning author Karina Fabian, these guides combine decades of professional experience, honest lessons learned, and a healthy dose of encouragement. You don't have to master everything at once. Just pick the boost you need, apply it, and keep moving forward.

## KEEP IN TOUCH

If you want to learn about future books, please

- Sign up for my newsletter. https://fabianspace.substack.com/subscribe Get short stories, updates, and a free book!
- Visit my website at https://karinafabian.com
- Follow me on Facebook: https://www.facebook.com/Karina-Fabian-Speculative-Fiction-with-a-Grin-2233839790277963

# ABOUT THE AUTHOR

Karina Fabian is an award-winning novelist, speaker, and stand-up comedian who has spent decades telling stories in as many ways as she can manage, from space-faring nuns to dragon private investigators. She's written over 50 science fiction and fantasy novels, plus short stories and humorous works.

In addition to writing fiction, she teaches workshops and webinars for beginning writers, sharing the lessons she's learned through success, trial and error, and stubborn perseverance. She believes you can take the craft seriously without taking yourself too seriously—and that writing is at its best when skill, heart, and a little bit of laughter work together.

Karina lives on Merritt Island with her husband, two of her four kids, two dogs, and a menagerie of imaginary friends who all want to tell her their stories.

# THERE'S MORE FUN IN FABIANSPACE!

**Science Fiction**

**Space Traipse: Hold My Beer**: Redneck ingenuity and common sense in a Star Trek-ish universe. Enjoy the adventures of the *HMB Impulsive*.

**The Rescue Sisters**: Intrepid women doing dangerous missions in space for the love of God and humankind.

**The Old Man and the Void**: Dex hunts relics on the edge of the black hole, and bags the catch of a lifetime.

**Jovian Heat**: As the next Great Storm of Jupiter rises, Cass must find the father of a baby in peril—but the father died before the child was conceived.

**Fantasy**

**DragonEye Story**: Vern's a snarky dragon on the wrong side of the Interdimensional Gap, solving crimes, battling evil, and saving the universes on an all-too-regular basis.

**Madness of Kanaan**: Deryl isn't crazy; he's psychic, and aliens of two worlds thinks he can save them. Maybe he can—but can he regain his sanity in the process?

**Horror**

**Neeta Lyffe, Zombie Exterminator**: Neeta's an average exterminator, taking out bugs, rodents, and the undead. Can she keep her friends alive, pay her bills, and find romance?

**Frightliner and Other Tales of the Supernatural (with Colleen Drippé)**: Truck-driving vampires terrorizing the road, Southern women doing what needs doing, a zombie wedding—a great story collection for horror lovers.

www.ingramcontent.com/pod-product-compliance
Lightning Source LLC
LaVergne TN
LVHW010659110826
845149LV00014B/3169

* 9 7 8 1 9 5 6 4 8 9 2 9 3 *